# SpringerBriefs in Criminology

## Translational Criminology

To Ralph.

A great colleague and a greater friend. And the latter is much more important.

Your friend

Jerry

Oct 2017

More information about this series at http://www.springer.com/series/11178

Jerry H. Ratcliffe • Evan T. Sorg

# Foot Patrol

Rethinking the Cornerstone of Policing

 Springer

Jerry H. Ratcliffe
Department of Criminal Justice
Temple University
Philadelphia, PA, USA

Evan T. Sorg
Department of Law and Justice Studies
Rowan University
Glassboro, NJ, USA

ISSN 2192-8533                ISSN 2192-8541    (electronic)
SpringerBriefs in Criminology
ISSN 2194-6442                ISSN 2194-6450    (electronic)
Translational Criminology
ISBN 978-3-319-65246-7        ISBN 978-3-319-65247-4    (eBook)
DOI 10.1007/978-3-319-65247-4

Library of Congress Control Number: 2017949279

Printed on acid-free paper

This Springer imprint is published by Springer Nature
The registered company is Springer International Publishing AG
The registered company address is: Gewerbestrasse 11, 6330 Cham, Switzerland

# Acknowledgments

Across two citywide randomized experiments and many studies before and after, we would like to gratefully acknowledge the invaluable assistance of the following people, all of whom are colleagues, coauthors, and friends: Elizabeth Groff, Jennifer Wood, Travis Taniguchi, Cory Haberman, Lallen Johnson, Caitlin Taylor, and Ralph Taylor. Their insights and wisdom have made us better scholars. A huge thanks also go to the hundreds of Philadelphia Police officers who shared their views and experiences with us and insights that made the bulk of this book possible. The level of dedication they demonstrate to the city and its citizens never ceases to astound us.

The Philadelphia Foot Patrol Experiment and Philadelphia Policing Tactics Experiment would not have been possible without the leadership of Police Commissioner (ret.) Charles Ramsey, Deputy Commissioner (ret.) Nola Joyce, Police Commissioner Rich Ross, Deputy Commissioner (ret.) Kevin Bethel, Deputy Commissioner (ret.) Tommy Wright, and all of the commanders and officers of the Philadelphia Police Department. We would also like to specially recognize Anthony D'Abruzzo and Kevin Thomas for their work behind the scenes during these collaborative experiments.

In the preparation of this manuscript, we would like to thank Cynthia Lum, D. Kim Rossmo, Renée Mitchell, Josh Koehnlein, and, from Springer, Katie Chabalko.

# Contents

# About the Authors

**Dr. Jerry H. Ratcliffe** is Professor of Criminal Justice and Director of the Center for Security and Crime Science at Temple University, Philadelphia. He served for over a decade as a police officer with London's Metropolitan Police (UK), has a Ph.D. from the University of Nottingham, and is a Fellow of the Royal Geographical Society. He was the lead researcher on the Philadelphia Foot Patrol Experiment and has published over 80 research articles and five books in the areas of intelligence-led policing, spatial analysis, criminal intelligence, and crime science. He has been a research adviser to both the Philadelphia Police Commissioner and to the Criminal Investigative Division of the FBI. He recently completed an experiment examining predictive policing strategies.

**Dr. Evan T. Sorg** is an Assistant Professor of Law and Justice Studies at Rowan University, an affiliated instructor and researcher in the Center for Security and Crime Science at Temple University, and a former New York City police officer. He served as a research assistant on the Philadelphia Foot Patrol Experiment during his PhD work at Temple. He has published several research articles on the topics of hot spots policing and crime analysis, three of which involve the topic of foot patrol, and stemmed from the Philadelphia Foot Patrol Experiment. He has taught numerous cohorts of police officers and crime analysts on the topic of crime mapping and crime analysis, and he teaches Central American police commanders on the topic of intelligence-led policing.

# Crowd-Pleasers and Crime Fighters

In 1960, Chicago was rocked by the Summerdale scandal. Eight Chicago cops enabled local thief Richard Morrison to burgle locations in the Summerdale police district on Chicago's north side. The officers not only acted as a lookout for the thief but also used their squad cars to transport stolen goods from the scene (Benzkofer 2013). The case resulted in the arrest and conviction of the officers, as well as the retirement of Police Commissioner Timothy O'Connor. Mired in controversy, Chicago turned to renowned police academic and practitioner O.W. Wilson as the city's next police chief. One of the first things he did to try and restore community trust was assign foot beat officers to each district. As Skogan and colleagues pointed out, this was largely a public relations exercise: "Not much was expected of these officers; they were to be *crowd-pleasers*" (Skogan et al. 1999: 76, emphasis added).

Are foot patrol officers just crowd-pleasers? Officers on foot have been the backbone of policing for the majority of the nearly 200-year history of the modern police service though, as we will discuss later, less so in recent decades. There is general agreement that officers on foot are central to police-community relations and positive neighborhood contacts: "Foot patrol is a pillar of community policing that stands alone in its simplicity and its impact on communal feelings of fear of violent crimes... The presence of a single officer can bring relief to a troubled sector and give its populace a new peace of mind" (Giannetti 2007: 22). And while not exactly the dominant policing model, foot patrols are widespread. In 2007 (the year most recently reported for foot patrol), the majority of police departments in the United States used regularly scheduled foot patrols (55%). This number rose to 81% for cities with over half a million residents, and 92% for cities with a million or more people (Reaves 2010).

Foot patrol is interesting because it changes the nature of social interactions between individuals. It slows the pace of approach, allowing an officer to take the time to assess the person or group she is drawing near to, and it draws individuals much closer together. On a busy city sidewalk, we pass within a breath of each other, sometimes brushing against fellow travelers. On quieter streets with few pedestrians, we might say good morning to the other person. As one sergeant

© The Author(s) 2017
J.H. Ratcliffe, E.T. Sorg, *Foot Patrol*, SpringerBriefs in Criminology,
DOI 10.1007/978-3-319-65247-4_1

reported to Cowell and Kringen (2016: 20), "People are more comfortable going up to an officer walking by them, shoulder to shoulder on the street, than they are to approach a cruiser." Because police officers on foot draw near other people at a much closer proximity than in a vehicle, there is an increase in "approachability," a concept that is difficult to define yet important to community/police relations (Mackenzie and Whitehouse 1995). As Weisburd et al. (2015) note, because these social processes work at a microlevel, there are opportunities for officers to lower the scale of social interactions and intervene in a positive way at the street level. Of course, officers can choose to wear sunglasses that conceal where they are looking and patrol with a permanent scowl, which will most likely negate any community interaction; therefore, as we discuss later in the book, choosing the right officers for the task (especially volunteers where possible) is as important as deciding to implement a foot patrol program.

Approachability seems to be associated with notions of trust and a sense of familiarity. It may also, therefore, be as important to assign the same officers to an area as it is to maintain a general policy of foot patrols. When familiarity does exist, it seems to work both ways. In a survey of officers in one county police department, officers on foot beats reported an increased sense of job satisfaction compared to officers in other forms of patrol, and they attributed less fear of crime to residents (Hayeslip and Cordner 1987). Yet for all the value of foot patrol, one of the major changes across the history of policing was the move from foot patrol to the use of squad cars. Informal contacts between the community and the police decreased, police became isolated, and community relations were harmed (Esbensen 1987).

Foot patrol officers are what some have called "proximity units" (Montolio and Planells-Struse 2015: 74), officers that have increased visibility and contact with the community, local businesses, and neighbors, and have an enhanced ability to learn about their concerns and security needs. Cars reduce proximity between people, irrespective of geographical distance. In their study of policing in Barcelona, Montolio and Planells-Struse (2015) concluded that people who had not been a victim of crime responded positively when stopped by the police, resulting in a lower crime risk perception for the area. Conversely, there was also some evidence that people who perceived that they were at risk of crime victimization increased their sense of insecurity after a random contact with the police. They concluded that "Stopping citizens and interacting with them can have an important impact on levels of security, making citizens feel safer" (Montolio and Planells-Struse 2015: 89).

Walking is good for us. Over 50 years ago, a London doctor discovered that conductors who spent all day climbing the stairs of double-decker buses had fewer heart attacks than the drivers who sat all day in the same buses, and mailmen on their routes had fewer heart attacks than clerks. Studies have shown that an average of 21 minutes a day of gentle perambulation can cut the risk of heart disease by 30% (Rubenstein 2015). One innovative police department "actually sees foot patrol as an opportunity for officers to de-stress. If an officer experiences a particularly stressful call, sergeants are empowered to place that officer on an immediate foot patrol assignment to provide them with an opportunity to de-escalate and de-stress through positive interactions with the community" (Cowell and Kringen 2016: 28). Walking can help to maintain brain volume and ward off cognitive decline in older age and can help to combat depression (Rubenstein 2015). Yet within policing, walking is often loathed: "The reason police officers are resistant to foot patrol is that they don't like it. It's the bottom of the barrel. It's tough work. And when it rains, you're likely to get wet" (Moskos 2008: 198–199).

Both authors of this book have had that experience. Ratcliffe started his policing career with the Metropolitan Police on H district in the East End of London (UK) on foot patrol in the areas of Mile End and Bow Road. He also worked foot patrol in Central London in and around Charing Cross. Sorg spent the beginning of his law enforcement career walking various foot posts in the 122nd Precinct in Staten Island, as well as occasional special details involving foot posts in Manhattan and Brooklyn, with the New York City Police Department (NYPD). Some of the opinions in this book (mainly in the last chapter) are therefore derived from the personal experiences of the authors enhanced by our involvement with the foot patrol experiments described later in this book and our reading of the literature. But opinions they remain, and we caution the reader appropriately. In the last chapter, we have tried to provide practical guidelines for the implementation of foot patrol and would prefer that these were drawn purely from the research surrounding foot patrol. Yet given how fundamental foot patrol has been to policing over the last two centuries, it is surprising how little we know about its effects. Weak as it is, we are able to summarize the majority of the existing knowledge comfortably in a single chapter. The absence of robust studies that combine conceptual clarity and methodological rigor means that we don't know as much as we should. Later in this book, we report in depth on two randomized controlled experiments that examined foot patrol (studies in which the authors were involved); however, given that most police officers around the world have spent at least some time on a foot beat, the absence of wisdom regarding if and how this patrol strategy affects crime and public opinion is alarming.

It might be that the effects are difficult to quantify. Police departments have an almost religious fervor around recording "official" activities such as traffic tickets, arrests, pedestrian investigations, and vehicle searches. But no paperwork would likely be generated to record the activities of officers in Philadelphia's 22nd district as they:

walk by barbershops, corner grocers, storefront churches, parks adorned with folk-art sculptures, domino tournaments under tarp gazebos and makeshift backboards mailed to telephone poles. They kick soccer balls with kids and banter about the weather with grandmothers cradling babies on rickety front porches, ignoring the hard looks from young men with pointy beards and neck tattoos. (Rubenstein 2015: 79)

If this is crowd-pleasing community work that is deemed valuable, then most police departments do a poor job of gathering evidence of this type of activity. Community interaction is rarely deemed important enough to formally record in administrative databases. As a result, we are not in a position to quantify the community engagement value of foot patrol.

Foot beat officers may also have a crime-fighting role that complements the crowd-pleasing one. Officers on foot have a significant sensory advantage over car-bound colleagues. For example, Dempsey suggests that there is even value in the sense of smell. He argues that clandestine illicit drug laboratories can be first noticed by their aroma, such that this fact "may allow an officer to develop the probable cause necessary to obtain a search warrant" (Dempsey 1992: 34). He is also enthusiastic about the opportunity to use hearing to detect faint sounds that would not be detected in a car. A multitude of senses is available to foot beats who want to better appreciate their immediate environment. As Ariel and colleagues note, "There may well be a critical aspect of deterrence provided by foot patrol which is missed in vehicle-based patrols: direct and proximate co-presence of power-holders and members of the public" (Ariel et al. 2016).

Most importantly, officers on foot have more time to assess what is going on around them. Regardless of the tempo of the street activity, foot beat officers can take more time to implement good decisions. Traffic stops are selective, and it is easy to tune out what is occurring around the police car; however, foot patrol is an immersive activity with potential human contact everywhere. As such, officers on foot make many more decisions about who they interact with either informally or formally. These choices are important for determining the tempo and character of the space the officers occupy. As Millie notes:

> Every police action, or inaction, sends a powerful message to its recipient and to wider audiences about who belongs within a society and about their place (or lack thereof) within its extant social hierarchies. How policing is carried out thus operates as a sensitive and often highly charged indicator of how adequately any society attends to the security and well-being of its members – and, increasingly today, of its denizen non-members. This is why policing so often grabs people's attention and provokes such strong and conflicting emotions. This is why policing matters. (Millie 2014: 45)

There are of course limitations to foot patrols. With the introduction of the patrol vehicle, foot beats were considered old-fashioned, outmoded, and inefficient. Officers on foot cannot quickly get to emergency calls and are ill-suited to stop vehicles. They can't provide the rapid response that was deemed so important to modern policing in the 1950s and 1960s, albeit a rapid response that was later shown to have no impact on the level of crime. But by the time the research was in, the genie was out of the bottle, and vehicle patrols had become the norm. Officers on foot on one level recognize the community policing value of their work, yet they can also lament that they are not engaged in "real" police work. An officer's presence on foot may reduce crime, but it makes for a boring day when little is taking place. Most job candidates will probably mention some version of serving the public and deterring crime in their job interview, but once in the role, officers quickly recognize that dealing with actual crime and disorder is much more interesting.

One frequently ignored crime-fighting role is the gathering of information that can feed intelligence-led policing. Sharp and attentive officers can generate a huge store of knowledge regarding an area, often in a short period of time. The slower pace that so many officers lament is perfect for taking in the tempo of a place and the people therein. That ability to interact with people on a nonthreatening day-to-day basis provides great opportunities to develop community contacts, criminal informants, and to learn where the nooks and crannies of a district are located. These are the hidden places away from prying eyes where kids go to smoke pot, addicts go to shoot up, and drunks wile away the hours. Criminal intelligence is vital in uncovering the intricacies of a police district and the criminal opportunities it holds; intelligence that can lead to the sort of quality arrests that officers are interested in making. Crime reduction associated with uniformed foot patrol is centered on the theory of deterrence or, in the sometimes esoteric language of criminologists, "uniformed power-holders who can make arrests for criminal transgressions that they detect cause rational actors to become substantially less likely to commit crime. Police powers of arrest and legal authority to apply necessary force create a threat to anyone contemplating a crime" (Ariel et al. 2016: 3). As Ariel and colleagues have demonstrated, some sort of uniform presence can be enough, even if not provided by the formal "police," if that presence signals the likelihood that police will be summoned. During a hot spots experiment in Peterborough, British Police Community Support Officers (civilian police staff members who wear a uniform but have limited powers in that they cannot make arrests, conduct searches of suspects, or carry weapons) on foot were able to cause a significant reduction in crime.

There are many aspects to the foot patrol policing of our society that we will cover in this short book. The next chapter reviews the literature on patrol work with a focus on foot patrol, and this leads us into a chapter that concentrates on two significant randomized controlled field experiments in foot patrol, the Philadelphia Foot Patrol Experiment and the Philadelphia Policing Tactics Experiment. The first of these Philadelphia studies suggests a crime-fighting role for foot patrol beyond the crowd-pleasing one so often associated with foot beats. However, the second advises that more caution is required, suggesting that the success of foot patrol is more nuanced. The chapter that follows delves more deeply into the lived experiences of foot patrol officers, frequently in their own words drawn from our field observations and interviews. We conclude the book with a chapter that draws together the strands of our book into a focus on practical foot patrol policies that police departments may wish to consider should they choose to deploy officers on foot.

## References

Ariel, B., Weinborn, C., & Sherman, L. W. (2016). "Soft" policing at hot spots—Do police community support officers work? A randomized controlled trial. *Journal of Experimental Criminology, 12*(3), 277–317.

Benzkofer, S. (2013). The Summerdale Scandal and the case of the babbling burglar. July 07. *Chicago Tribune.*

Cowell, B. M., & Kringen, A. L. (2016). *Engaging communities one step at a time: Policing's tradition of foot patrol as an innovative community engagement strategy* (p. 51). Washington, D.C.: Police Foundation.

Dempsey, T. (1992). *Contemporary patrol tactics.* Englewood Cliffs: Prentice Hall.

Esbensen, F.-A. (1987). Foot patrols: Of what value? *American Journal of Police, 6*(1), 45–65.

Giannetti, W. J. (2007). What is operation safe streets? *IALEIA Journal, 17*(1), 22–32.

Hayeslip, D. W., Jr., & Cordner, G. W. (1987). Effects of community-oriented patrol on police officer attitudes. *The American Journal of Police, 6*(1), 95–119.

Mackenzie, I. K., & Whitehouse, R. (1995). The approachability of police officers patrolling on foot: A pilot study. *Policing and Society, 5*(4), 339–347.

Millie, A. (2014). What are the police for? Re-thinking policing post-austerity. In J. M. Brown (Ed.), *The future of policing* (pp. 52–63). New York: Routledge.

Montolio, D., & Planells-Struse, S. (2015). When police patrols matter: The effect of police proximity on citizens' crime risk perception. *Journal of Economic Psychology, 50*, 73–93.

Moskos, P. (2008). *Cop in the hood: My year policing Baltimore's Eastern District*. Princeton: Princeton University Press.

Reaves, B. A. (2010). *Local police departments, 2007* (p. 41). Washington, D.C.: Bureau of Justice Statistics.

Rubenstein, D. (2015). *Born to walk*. Toronto: ECW Press.

Skogan, W. G., Hartnett, S. M., DuBois, J., Comey, J. T., Kaiser, M., & Lovig, J. H. (1999). *On the beat: Police and community problem solving*. Boulder: Westview Press.

Weisburd, D., Davis, M., & Gill, C. (2015). Increasing collective efficacy and social capital at crime hot spots: New crime control tools for police. *Policing: A Journal of Policy and Practice, 9*(3), 265–274.

# A History of Foot Patrol

## Introduction

Generations of police officers have performed foot patrols. In previous lives, both of your current authors walked beats across the pond from one another. From the American colonists who patrolled in the night watch to the millennials walking beats today, foot patrolling has remained a cornerstone of policing. Despite the enduring nature of its practice, the rationale underlying police foot patrols, and indeed the mission of foot patrol officers, has not been static. Peel's Bobbies sought to provide an "unremitting watch" (Shearing 1996: 74)—patrolling in a highly visible fashion and conveying to would-be criminals that their illegal activities would not go unnoticed. Conversely, community policing officers walking the beat during the 1980s and 1990s had a primary mission of winning the hearts and minds of the community and mending the police-community relationship that had soured in the preceding decades. Crime took a backseat to police legitimacy. More recently in Philadelphia, police administrators have rediscovered Peel's original mission, but with greater geographic focus fueled by digital technology and grounded in academic research and theorizing that has emerged since the formation of Peel's Metropolitan Police. Partly as a result of the work in Philadelphia (described in greater detail in the next chapter), departments around the world have begun to reimagine how police foot patrols might fit into their organizational strategies and support their organizational mission.

Before moving to the contemporary use of foot patrols in Philadelphia in the chapters that follow, this chapter tells the historical story of foot patrol, how its use has waxed and waned through the generations, and how various events in the history of law enforcement have shaped its practice. We begin by briefly walking readers through the evolution of various systems of law enforcement that preceded the development of government police agencies as we know them today. These archetype methods of policing relied heavily on foot patrols and provided important first steps toward establishing public police agencies. After discussing how foot patrol

© The Author(s) 2017
J.H. Ratcliffe, E.T. Sorg, *Foot Patrol*, SpringerBriefs in Criminology,
DOI 10.1007/978-3-319-65247-4_2

was a central component of the strategies of the London "Met," we then trace the various eras in American policing and the role that foot patrols had (or did not have) during each. We will examine the evaluation research evidence on foot patrol from the seminal Newark Foot Patrol Experiment and the studies that followed, and how the findings from Newark drove foot patrol to be considered a cornerstone of the emergent community policing movement—findings that appear especially relevant today in the wake of community unrest in cities like Baltimore, Charlotte, and Ferguson. Finally, we trace relevant theorizing concerned with the criminology of place and how the associated research has transformed the thinking of academics and police leaders alike. We close by discussing how these theoretical and empirical developments led the Philadelphia Police Department to refine and retest the crime reduction benefits of foot patrol with two large-scale randomized trials beginning in 2009.

## Humble Beginnings

The Metropolitan Police Act of 1829 established the world's first modern public police force. Sir Robert Peel, the British Home Secretary and architect of the legislation, would come to be known as the father of modern policing given the profound effects that his vision would have on law enforcement around the world. Although the Metropolitan Police that he created would come to be the first formal law enforcement agency as a result of this legislation, law enforcement had taken place in various forms around the world for centuries. In both Greece and Rome, for example, magistrates were appointed and tasked with enforcing the law until the third-century BCE and the sixth-century BCE, respectively. By 6 CE, a force of *praefectus urbi*, the first paid law enforcement officers, were responsible for patrolling Rome on foot (Kunkel 1973). After the decline of the Roman Empire, Europe's feudal monarchies took responsibility for their own law enforcement, largely relying upon a night watch system wherein men walked the town to ensure peace and address signs of trouble (Worrall and Schmalleger 2016).

Nowhere was this better exemplified than in post-Norman conquest England, where night watches would evolve into the frankpledge system, a community-based system of law enforcement that also relied on foot patrols (Peak 2009). Although this frankpledge system would survive for centuries, these private law enforcement arrangements—systems that relied heavily on unpaid community members—would begin to fall out of favor by the 1800s. Although public funds had been used to pay watchmen to a limited extent in previous centuries, this would begin to change. Perhaps most notably, John and Henry Fielding, two London magistrates, began to pay their men to serve as constables and provide London with a nighttime patrol (Armitage 1932). In addition to performing investigations for the Fielding brothers, these *Bow Street Runners* would patrol London streets on foot and provide patrols on horseback in outskirts of the city (Worrall and Schmalleger 2016).

While foot patrols had been a cornerstone of virtually all systems of law enforcement that preceded even the first modern police department, the purpose of these early foot patrols was to be reactive and served largely as a means of apprehending law violators and searching for crimes in progress. Sir Robert Peel had a different vision for his constables, and prevention would be at the heart of the police mission in London.

## Peel's Great Experiment

For Peel and the first two commissioners of the Metropolitan Police, Sir Richard Mayne and Colonel Sir Charles Rowan, crime prevention was seen as the primary objective that police should strive to attain. Mayne and Rowan wrote in 1829 that:

> The primary object of an efficient police is the prevention of crime; the next that of detection of punishment of offenders if crime is committed. To these ends, all the efforts of police should be directed. (as cited in Faulkner 2006: 256)

To achieve this deterrent mission, constables were outfitted with a distinct blue coat and pants, given a black top hat, armed with a truncheon (a short baton), and provided a rattle for raising an alarm to their fellow constables if necessary (Radzinowicz 1948). These constables were assigned to one of the 17 new divisions, each based on the geographic distribution of crime. Each division was commanded by a superintendent, and below him along the chain of command were 4 inspectors, 16 sergeants, and 165 constables (Peak 2009). Constables had the responsibility of providing foot patrols in the city.

Whether or not Peel actually articulated his oft-quoted principles of policing (Lentz and Chaires 2007), they have nevertheless become ingrained in the minds of students and scholars of law enforcement. Many of these principles, and indeed the managerial philosophy of the Met Police, drew heavily on the deterrence doctrine that scholars like Beccaria (1963 [1764]) had voiced in the previous century. At the most basic level, in order to deter would-be criminals from committing a crime, Beccaria and others theorized that the risk of apprehension had to appear great, and the prospect of being punished should one be apprehended must be certain and swiftly applied. It is clear that the emergent Metropolitan Police adhered to this deterrence doctrine. Constables in the Met played a central role in conveying the first variable in the deterrence equation. By deploying constables in uniform, Peel, Mayne, and Rowan hoped to convey to criminals that the costs of crime outweighed the benefits—that the risk of apprehension was far too great to justify becoming involved in illegal activities. The cornerstone of their approach was random foot patrols that would capitalize on a perception of omnipresence. The Metropolitan Police's ubiquitous use of foot patrol would serve as the benchmark for professional policing in many countries, and among these were the emerging urban police departments in the United States.

## The Early Days of American Policing

Much like the developments in law enforcement in Europe, policing in colonial American followed a progression that eventually led to the establishment of public police agencies by the mid-1800s. As was the case in Europe, early American urban policing relied upon a watch comprised of civilian men who patrolled cities on foot in search of fires, crime, and disorder (Walker and Katz 2013). Unfortunately, law enforcement in the United States would soon be exposed for being an ineffective and inefficient system. Watches were often understaffed and lacked the appropriate personnel to patrol, quell disobedience, or investigate crimes, and crime reporting systems were largely nonexistent. As immigration increased, American cities became crowded and more dangerous, and because the sheriff and watchmen were paid fees garnered from providing civil and criminal enforcement, they were much more apt to pursue their civil enforcement responsibilities to maximize personal return (Greenberg 1976). The failure of the watch system in the United States and the rising crime rates in American cities led political establishments to replicate Peel's model of policing in London, and by the mid-1800s, America was entering what is commonly referred to as the political era of policing.

## *The Political Era*

Given the lasting stain that slave patrols in the South have left on the history of policing in America (Reichel 1988), it is not surprising that the development of the first modern metropolitan law enforcement agencies in the United States had problems from the start. While the first agencies in places like New York, Philadelphia, and Boston were modeled on London's Metropolitan Police, early efforts to establish legitimate public police forces fell flat, and little difference from the night watches of old was evident. There were several reasons for these failures, yet political influence and patronage were chief among them. Unlike the men and women who are subject to lengthy hiring procedures and background investigations before joining police agencies today, officers working during the political era needed only be politically connected to secure a job. For example, a payment of $300 to the infamous Tammany Hall was enough to secure a law enforcement position in New York City (Berman and Berman 1987). There were no hiring standards, no automatic disqualifying factors as we understand them today, and no formal training for officers. Upon a change in political regime, it was not uncommon for an entire police force to be fired and replaced.

Police agencies were ineffective, inefficient, and corrupt. During this era, foot beats remained the primary form of police patrols. Yet in cities like Chicago, officers performed foot patrols on beats that were up to 4 miles long, so any deterrent value that these foot patrol officers may have had was minimal—a far cry from the intended sense of omnipresence that Peel had envisaged (Walker and Katz 2013).

Indeed, these patrols hardly served the public interest and were more a position that corrupt officers used for personal gain. Supervision ranged from weak to nonexistent, and officers oftentimes either shirked their duties, preferring to spend time in barbershops or saloons (Lardner and Reppetto 2001), or actively colluded with criminals—developing relationships and ignoring criminal behavior as part of quid pro quo arrangements (Schneider 1980). Although trivial attempts at reform did arise during this time, the political era of policing is largely seen as a flawed attempt at introducing a formalized system of law enforcement in America.

## The Professional Era and the Decline of Foot Patrols

For all of the failures that were realized during the political era of policing, the professional era of policing stands in stark contrast. The professional era coincided with the broader political movement of progressivism, and the regulation of various social institutions was a central component (Walker 1977). The police "professionalization movement" fits nicely into progressivism's philosophy, and so it is no surprise that specific agenda items from the professionalization movement would slowly be realized from 1900 to 1960 (Walker and Katz 2013: 34). The most notable leader of this movement was August Vollmer who, along with other reformers such as his protégé O.W. Wilson, sought the removal of political influence and the development of efficient, properly managed police agencies as vital to improving the American system of law enforcement.

Vollmer began his police career as the Marshal of Berkeley, California, which had a force of only three men. After successfully lobbying city council for an increase in his force (from 3 to 12 officers), he gained a degree of notoriety for being the first chief to order his men to patrol on bike rather than on foot. Vollmer's experiments with rapid response revealed that officers responding on bicycle reached their callers up to three times faster than officers patrolling on foot (Douthit 1975). Before the widespread adoption of police patrol cars, the seeds for classifying foot patrol as an obsolete and inefficient practice were already being sown by Vollmer.

Vollmer and other reformers advocated for organizational changes and the incorporation of best management practices in policing, more stringent standards in hiring personnel, and for educational requirements, including college degrees (Walker 1998). Although these and other reforms would not take hold overnight, Vollmer would leave behind a legacy that would have lasting impacts on the profession during the decades that followed. Many of these reforms were undoubtedly positive ones, and political influence was lessened by a substantial degree.

When Peel was implementing his vision for professional public police agencies in London, a hierarchical structure, the donning of military-like uniforms, rank designations, and an authoritarian system of command were all borrowed from military models. American police agencies would also appropriate these emblems as part of a professionalization movement that focused squarely on improving the management of police agencies. Yet this led to a new police subculture that embraced a military ethos, resisted reforms, and became insulated and isolated from the community (Walker 1977). An emphasis on law and order and crime control likewise diminished the legitimacy of the service role that many officers and agencies had previously embodied. Not surprisingly, the "crime-fighter image"—the idea that police are most often involved in fighting crime and chasing and apprehending criminals—became solidified as a result of this emphasis. To this day, police are frequently eager to embrace this image, and police culture has come to value this crime-fighting work—a good collar or a successful chase—while providing services, solving problems, and working to improve the perceived legitimacy of the police by the community received far less respect (Wood et al. 2014). It is not surprising that foot patrol became seen as rather pedestrian (no pun intended) and out of kilter with the ethos of a fast-moving, crime-fighting police department.

New (for the time) technology supported reformers' emphasis on efficiency, and radio communications, the telephone and 911 systems, and the patrol car would revolutionize policing (Walker 1984). It would also give rise to what is referred to as the "standard model of policing," which emphasizes random routine police patrols in cars, rapid police response to 911 calls, and reactive investigations of crimes. In this environment, a move to vehicle-based patrols was inevitable. Cars were becoming a widespread form of transportation in the United States, and ordinary citizens and criminals alike were increasingly behind the wheel. Vehicle-based patrols were seen by police reformers as a way in which police could provide greater coverage of patrol, allowing police to quickly respond to calls for help. Many believed that vehicle-based patrols would more effectively deter crime, and by the 1960s, most cities had abandoned the foot patrols that had dominated policing for centuries and instead relied upon vehicle-based patrols to deter and apprehend criminals and control crime (Walker and Katz 2013).

## Conflicting Pressures Slowly Drive a Crisis in Policing

As the reforms that were introduced in the previous decades took hold, new problems emerged. Although the advent of the patrol car was seen by reformers as a positive step toward improving police efficiency, they failed to anticipate the negative consequences that this move elicited. Being isolated from the public only furthered the "us versus them" mentality brought on by the crime-fighter image and emphasis on crime control that police reforms had ushered in. Efforts to improve police management were largely not matched with parallel efforts to improve the police-community relationship. Minority communities, in particular, viewed the police as an "occupying force," and these tensions would ultimately result in a police-community relations crisis (Walker and Katz 2013: 38).

It would be naïve to write that the relationship between the police and communities of color only deteriorated during the professional era of policing, as little evidence suggests that the dynamics of this relationship had improved much since the time of slave patrols. It is a harsh reality that the police and minority communities have never had a particularly positive relationship across the country. Nevertheless, starting in the 1960s, the rest of the country began to learn what minority communities had known and experienced for too long: police brutality and abuse ran rampant in far too many communities. A series of riots, perhaps most notably the Watts riots, brought this conflict to the forefront of the American consciousness. Subsequently, a series of Supreme Court decisions would limit police powers and discretion, and a number of national reports were published which were critical of police and questioned the effectiveness of newly reformed police agencies. Juggling what were seen as the conflicting pressures of crime fighting and community engagement, and faced with a public dissatisfied with police performance on both fronts, many law enforcement agencies began to reconsider the utility of foot patrol.

## Policing Starts to Learn What Works

It must have been tough being a police chief in the middle of the last century. Faced with a failure of the hard-fought professionalization to contain public disappointment in police, and growing unrest among the civil rights and anti-Vietnam war communities, the police had adopted a standard model of policing that was completely untested. As crime rates, disorder, drug use, and civil unrest scourged the United States during the 1960s, police were faced with the uncomfortable realization that they may be losing the fight against crime. Since the time of Peel, police had assumed that patrol was an effective deterrent to crime, and yet, crime and disorder were escalating. The medical field was starting to make significant progress with evidence-based medicine, and, with a growing scholarly and practical appreciation of such approaches, the tenets of the standard model of policing would soon be subjected to the same types of empirical study. One of the most important studies executed during this time would directly test the crime reduction benefits of patrol, the backbone of policing since the time of Peel.

The now famous Kansas City Preventative Patrol Experiment (Kelling et al. 1974) is arguably one of the most influential studies conducted in policing. Yet, there were critics who had questioned the effectiveness of police patrols long before this landmark study. As early as 1930, scholars had questioned the efficacy of police patrols and concluded that patrol's effectiveness had no scientific basis (Walton 1958). By the 1960s, modest attempts at estimating the crime control benefits of police patrol were underway, but a number of constraints made high-quality evaluations difficult. Police were often reluctant to put their departments under scrutiny, crime data lacked quality and were not readily available, and early police researchers had some difficulty applying appropriate research methodologies to study the problem (Kelling et al. 1974). These obstacles would, to some degree, be overcome during the Kansas City experiment.

In the original report produced by the Police Foundation, Kelling and his colleagues (1974: iii–iv) noted that:

In 1971, the Kansas City Police Department had a chief with unusually long tenure -at that point ten years. The average length of service of police chiefs in major urban areas is less than half that. The chief in Kansas City was respected and supported by both the community and his officers. He was progressive and willing to innovate...By 1971, Chief Clarence M. Kelley said, "Many of us in the department had the feeling we were training, equipping, and deploying men to do a job neither we, nor anyone else, knew much about."

Your current authors know from our experience in Philadelphia the importance of partnering with leaders that are respected, innovative, and interested in answering questions about the effectiveness of their policies. With Chief Kelley in Kansas City, the conditions were ripe for a large-scale study of police patrol effectiveness, and with support from the Police Foundation, researchers and police worked together to design, execute, and evaluate the experiment. The slow emergence of research and the Kansas City experiment, in particular, would usher in a few police leaders who did not rely on intuition but instead were prepared to try different approaches and learn what works. For the first time in modern policing, empirical evidence would begin to play a role in tactical decision-making.

Because the experiment has become a part of policing lore, we need not cover it in depth here. Very briefly, 15 police beats in Kansas City were randomly placed into three conditions: (1) five beats were deemed reactive beats where officers did not perform patrols and only responded to calls for service; (2) in five beats (the control beats), business went on as usual, and the normal dosage of police patrols was applied; and (3) in five beats the dosage of police patrols was increased about threefold through the application of extra resources to provide patrol coverage. The most important takeaway? None of the beats had any meaningful differences in the rate of crime. Put another way, regardless of whether random police patrols were increased three times, or whether they were removed completely, crime occurred at around the same volume—random, routine patrol did not seem to prevent crime as Peel and others had assumed.

The other two tenets of the standard model of policing did not fare any better when they were subject to empirical evaluation. Reducing response time to calls for police service did not appear to increase the likelihood of an arrest. It was soon determined that the majority of calls made to police were not actually "in progress" calls, and citizens often did not call the police for help right after being victimized (Bieck and Kessler 1977). And although crime victims deserve to have their assailants arrested and held responsible for their crimes, we learned during the research revolution that detectives were rarely the ones responsible for clearing a crime. In fact, it is most often the patrol officer on scene who collects the information that leads to an arrest, not the follow-up detective work that is oftentimes sensationalized on television (Greenwood and Petersilia 1975).

Two things became clear by the end of the 1970s: (1) the effectiveness of the strategies upon which police heavily relied appeared to be either nonexistent or exaggerated and (2) the police-community relationship had continued to sour to a worrisome degree. For these reasons, community policing became a hot topic in law enforcement circles, and the government would soon invest millions of dollars in departments wishing to implement a community policing model.

# Community Policing

Before community policing became a buzzword in law enforcement circles in the 1980s, team policing was an early attempt at decentralizing police agencies, working with communities in deciding police priorities, and improving the police-community relationship (Walker 1993). In 1967 the President's Commission on Law Enforcement and Administration of Justice endorsed the idea of team policing, yet by the end of the 1970s, the practice would fall into obscurity (Walker 1993; Greene 1987). Much like community policing, team policing sought to redefine the police role and move away from the standard model of policing. It aimed to focus police services at the neighborhood level, emphasized geographic accountability, and stressed the permanent assignment of teams of officers to specific neighborhoods to increase communications between the officers and the residents that they were serving (Greene 1987). Although team policing was largely thought of as a failure, community policing would emerge in the 1980s and attempt to achieve many of the same goals. Community foot patrols were a principal component of both philosophies.

Since the 1980s, community policing has been subjected to a great deal of empirical evaluation (albeit of low methodological rigor), and the components of this organizational philosophy have been articulated in numerous volumes and texts (Skogan and Hartnett 1997; Skogan 2006b; Wilson 2006; Trojanowicz and Bucqueroux 1998). But during the 1980s, it was still an emerging idea, and as Greene (1987: 1) observed at the time, "community policing means many things to many people." Arguably, this remains the case. Even today, community policing is a word thrown around by laymen who do not have a robust understanding of the many intricacies involved in *true* community policing models.

Wes Skogan (2006a, b: 5–6), today one of the most well-known names connected to community policing, notes that:

> It [community policing] is an organizational strategy that leaves setting priorities and the means of achieving them largely to residents and the police who serve their neighborhoods. Community policing is a process rather than a product. Across the nation it has proved to have three core strategic components: decentralization, citizen involvement, and problem solving. In practices, these three dimensions are densely interrelated. Departments that shortchange even one of them will not field a very effective program.

To this day, many departments claim to be doing community policing without actually following through with the strategic necessities that Skogan describes. They point to individual projects and operational tactics as evidence of their commitment to engaging in community policing without necessarily adopting the overarching philosophy. Foot patrol programs are one such example. Simply deploying police personnel on foot does not make a community policing program, but it has nevertheless become a deployment scheme that is synonymous with community policing. This is perhaps unsurprising. Greene (1987) argues that three strains of police operational practice and philosophy pushed police agencies toward the adoption of foot patrol programs in the 1980s.

First, the growth of research discussed above, and the loss of faith in the tenets of the standard model of policing that it brought, led to a perception that nothing works and that "the police do not prevent crime" (Bayley 1994: 3). As the presumption that police work carried out under the standard model deterred crime was shattered, the police sought other means to demonstrate that their work was effective. Second, problem-oriented policing specifically (Goldstein 1979), and the general notion that police should focus on resolving problems in communities rather than strictly focus on crime prevention, arose during this time. This was fueled by a new emphasis on improving the quality of life of citizens and reducing their fear of crime. And finally, and perhaps most importantly, the link between disorder and fear that Wilson and Kelling (1982) famously raised (in their broken windows hypothesis) led many agencies to consider whether attacking citizens' perceptions of crime and disorder was a fruitful strategy. With findings from the seminal Newark Foot Patrol Experiment suggesting that foot patrols could, in fact, reduce citizens' fear of crime and perceptions of crime and disorder (Kelling et al. 1981), these perceptions became the target of interventions in some agencies.

## Experimenting with Foot Patrol

Although vehicle patrols replaced foot patrol to a significant degree, foot patrols never disappeared. In some jurisdictions, foot patrols were used due to economic constraints, such as the cost of gasoline, and others began increasing foot patrols in response to pressure from the public and the need to improve police-community relations (Kelling et al. 1981). The general consensus among police practitioners and scholars during the time just before the Newark Foot Patrol Experiment was that although some benefits of foot patrol existed, the disadvantages far outweighed them to justify their widespread adoption (Iannone 1975). Nevertheless, some agencies revisited placing greater numbers of officers on foot.

Pendland and Gay (1972) reported that in Fort Worth, a foot patrol program reduced reported crime and increased citizen satisfaction with police services. During a team policing experiment, Bloch and Ulberg (1972) reported that the police-community relationship was improved and that foot patrol was an especially popular aspect of this effort. However most evaluations of foot patrol programs that preceded the work in Newark reported inconsistent findings or lacked methodological rigor. With a renewed interest in foot patrol that emerged after the research revolution and in light of the police-community relations crisis, the Newark Foot Patrol Experiment sought to robustly examine the impacts that foot patrol had on crime, perceptions of crime and disorder, and citizen satisfaction.

The findings of the Newark experiment would encourage the community policing movement and inspire a reemergence of foot patrol in departments around the country, yet the first major finding supported the results of the Kansas City experiment that had occurred a few years before. Foot patrol did not seem to influence actual levels of crime. When comparisons were made between beats treated with foot patrol and those acting as controls, no meaningful differences arose. The Newark experiment reinforced the notion that police patrols were unable to influence crime itself.

Fortunately, other findings from Newark pointed to several positive benefits of foot patrol that were not realized with vehicle patrols. In Kansas City, not only were vehicle patrols found to be ineffective, they also were not noticed by citizens. That was not the case with foot patrol in Newark. Citizens reported that they were aware of the foot patrols. Further, although they did not actually influence levels of crime, citizens that were surveyed believed that the foot patrols were working and reported that the severity of crime problems in the foot patrol beats were diminishing. With a perception that crime problems were declining, citizens also were more likely to report feeling safe in foot patrol areas relative to non-foot beat areas. Finally, foot patrols resulted in citizens reporting higher levels of satisfaction with police services. So although actual levels of crime remained unchanged, it became clear that foot patrol had some positive benefits. With a police-community relations problem upon them, foot patrol seemed like a perfect solution to police legitimacy issues.

Realizing the potential value of foot patrols, the city of Boston completely restructured their patrol operations to make foot patrols the predominant form of policing. In a city that previously relied heavily on vehicle patrols (at the time they made up 80% of all units), this was a significant departure from their normal business model. After the restructuring, 34% of the city's patrol units were on foot, which left 24% of patrol being conducted by single-officer vehicle patrols. As was the case in Newark, results of an evaluation of this new deployment scheme found no crime reduction benefits (Bowers and Hirsch 1987). In the City of Flint (Michigan), police implemented a neighborhood foot patrol program in response to the Newark experiment, finding both a crime reduction benefit and positive reaction by the public. Although the methodology to evaluate the intervention in Flint had significant limitations (Bowers and Hirsch 1987), these and other evaluations resulted in foot patrol reemerging as a valid policing strategy in the eyes of police chiefs. They embraced the community relationship benefits and largely ignored the lack of crime control associated with foot beats. It is therefore little wonder that foot patrol came to play a significant role in the community policing movement that had emerged and would flourish during the 1990s.

## Rethinking the Unit of Analysis

As community policing became the predominant managerial philosophy of the 1980s and into the 1990s, a new group of scholars began reexamining whether the then solidified adage that the "police do not prevent crime" (Bayley 1998: 3) was accurate. Environmental criminology would emerge as an increasingly influential perspective in thinking about crime, and it would have significant impacts on the policing profession (Mastrofski et al. 2010). Perhaps the most notable study contributing to the birth of what is now known as "place-based policing" (Weisburd 2008) is the work of Lawrence Sherman and his colleagues (1989). With the assistance of relatively new mapping technology (at least as it related to the study of crime), it was found that crime was astoundingly concentrated. They found that relatively few crime "hot spots" existed and that these hot spots accounted for a bulk of the crime that was reported. For example, in Minneapolis only about 3% of places in the city accounted for 50% of calls for police service. This relationship strengthened when crime types were disaggregated. This concept has come to be known as the law of crime concentration (Weisburd 2015). Sherman and Weisburd (1995) would later test whether concentrating police patrols at these limited numbers of places could produce crime reductions. Was it that police had the unit of analysis wrong? Police had been randomly patrolling in large administrative boundaries such as beat or sectors since the time of Peel, but with the realization that the majority of places in these large beats experienced little or no crime, was it time for a different approach?

Findings, also from Minneapolis, suggested that conclusions regarding the absense of crime reduction effects of police patrols may have been premature. In a groundbreaking randomized control trial, Sherman and Weisburd (1995) found that a more geographically concentrated patrol—at hot spots—could reduce crime and disorder. During the experimental period, calls for police service declined from between 6% and 13%, and observed disorder was cut in half. It seemed that another look at the effects of police patrols was necessary, and in the decades that followed, multiple evaluations would demonstrate that hot-spot policing is an effective crime deterrent (Braga et al. 2014).

By the mid-2000s, numerous studies concluded that several tactics—general vehicle patrol, problem-oriented policing, and crackdowns—worked if introduced at crime hot spots. But what about foot patrol? As was the case in Kansas City three decades prior, there was a need to retest the crime reduction benefits of foot patrol, this time at crime hot spots. And in one part of the country, the necessary conditions were coalescing to enable a large-scale study. In 2007, new political leadership, led by an innovative mayor named Michael Nutter, would take control of Philadelphia (Pennsylvania). Police Commissioner Charles Ramsey, a major player in the community policing movement in Chicago, would be appointed by Nutter to take over the Philadelphia Police Department and address an emerging violence problem. As a respected leader, innovator, and empiricist, Ramsey would pilot the return of foot beats and then commit to a large-scale test of foot patrol during the summer of 2009, right when two large classes were set to graduate from the police academy. The next chapter examines these experiments conducted in Philadelphia under Commissioner Ramsey's leadership.

# References

Armitage, G. (1932). *The history of the Bow Street runners* (pp. 1729–1829). London: Wishart.

Bayley, D. H. (1994). *Police for the future.* New York: Oxford University Press.

Bayley, D. H. (1998). *Policing in America: Assessment and prospects.* Washington: Police Foundation.

Beccaria, C. (1963 [1764]). *On crimes and punishment* (trans: Paolucci, H.). Upper Saddle River: Prentice-Hall.

Berman, J. S., & Berman, J. S. (1987). *Police administration and progressive reform: Theodore Roosevelt as police commissioner of New York.* New York: Greenwood Press Westport, CT.

Bieck, W., & Kessler, D. A. (1977). *Response time analysis.* Washington, D.C.: Department of Justice.

Bloch, P. B., & Ulberg, C. (1972). The beat commander concept. *Police Chief, 39*(9), 55–63.

Bowers, W. J., & Hirsch, J. H. (1987). Impact of foot patrol staffing on crime and disorder in Boston: An unmet promise. *American Journal of Police, 6,* 17.

Braga, A. A., Papachristos, A. V., & Hureau, D. M. (2014). The effects of hot spots policing on crime: An updated systematic review and meta-analysis. *Justice Quarterly, 31*(4), 633–663.

Douthit, N. (1975). August Vollmer, Berkeley's first Chief of Police, and the emergence of police professionalism. *California Historical Quarterly California Historical Society Quarterly, 54*(2), 101–124.

Faulkner, D. (2006). *Crime, state and citizen: A field full of folk* (2nd ed.). Winchester: Waterside Press.

Goldstein, H. (1979). Improving policing: A problem-oriented approach. *Crime and Delinquency, 25*(2), 236–258.

Greenberg, D. (1976). *Crime and law enforcement in the colony of New York, 1691–1776.* Ithica: Cornell University Press.

Greene, J. R. (1987), Foot patrol and community policing: Past practices and future prospects. *American Journal of Police, 6*(1), 1–16.

Greenwood, P. W., & Petersilia, J. (1975). *The criminal investigation process, volume I: Summary and policy implications.* Santa Monica: Rand Corporation.

Iannone, N. F. (1975). *Principles of police patrol.* New York: McGraw-Hill.

Kelling, G. L., Pate, T., Dieckman, D., & Brown, C. E. (1974). *The Kansas City preventive patrol experiment.* Washington, D.C.: Police Foundation.

Kelling, G. L., Pate, A., Ferrara, A., Utne, M., & Brown, C. E. (1981). The Newark foot patrol experiment. Washington. In *D.C.: The Police Foundation.*

Kunkel, W. (1973). *An introduction to Roman legal and constitutional history.* Oxford: Clarendon Press.

Lardner, J., & Reppetto, T. (2001). *NYPD: A city and its police.* New York: Macmillan.

Lentz, S. A., & Chaires, R. H. (2007). The invention of Peel's principles: A study of policing 'text-book' history. *Journal of Criminal Justice, 35*(1), 69–79.

Mastrofski, S. D., Weisburd, D., & Braga, A. A. (2010). Rethinking policing: The policy implications of hot spots of crime. In N. A. Frost, J. D. Freilich, & T. R. Clear (Eds.), *Contemporary issues in criminal justice policy* (pp. 251–264). Belmont: Wadsworth, Cengage Learning.

Peak, K. J. (2009). *Policing America: Challenges and best practices.* Upper Saddle River: Pearson/Prentice Hall.

Pendland, M. B., & Gay, W. G. (1972). Foot patrols: The fort worth experience. *The Police Chief, 39*(4), 46–48.

Radzinowicz, L. (1948). *A history of English criminal law and its administration from 1750: The emergence of penal policy* (Vol. 5). London: Stevens & Sons.

Reichel, P. L. (1988). Southern slave patrols as a transitional police type. *American Journal of Police, 7,* 51.

Schneider, J. C. (1980). *Detroit and the problem of order, 1830–1880: A geography of crime, riot, and policing.* Lincoln: University of Nebraska Press.

Shearing, C. (1996). Reinventing police: Policing as governance. In F. Sack, M. Voss, D. Frehsee, A. Funk, & H. Reinke (Eds.), *Privatisierung Staalicker kontrolle: Befunde, Konzepte, tendenzen*. Baden-Baden: Nomos Verlagsgesellschaft.

Sherman, L., & Weisburd, D. (1995). General deterrent effects of police patrol in crime "hot spots": A randomized, controlled trial. *Justice Quarterly, 12*(4), 625–648.

Sherman, L. W., Gartin, P., & Buerger, M. E. (1989). Hot spots of predatory crime: Routine activities and the criminology of place. *Criminology, 27*(1), 27–55.

Skogan, W. G. (2006a). *Police and community in Chicago: A tale of three cities*. New York: Oxford University Press on Demand.

Skogan, W. G. (2006b). The promise of community policing. In D. Weisburd & A. A. Braga (Eds.), *Police innovation: Contrasting perspectives* (pp. 27–43). Chicago: Cambridge University Press.

Skogan, W. G., & Hartnett, S. M. (1997). *Community policing, Chicago style*. New York: Oxford University Press.

Trojanowicz, R. C., & Bucqueroux, B. (1998). *Community policing: How to get started*. Cincinnati: Routledge.

Walker, S. (1977). *A critical history of police reform*. Lexington: Lexington Books.

Walker, S. (1984). "Broken Windows" and fractured history: The use and misuse of history in recent police patrol analysis. *Justice Quarterly, 1*(1), 75–90.

Walker, S. (1993). Does anyone remember team policing-lessons of the team policing experience for community policing. *American Journal of Police, 12*(1), 33–56.

Walker, S. (1998). *Popular justice: A history of American criminal justice*. New York: Oxford University Press.

Walker, S., & Katz, C. M. (2013). *Police in America* (8th ed.). New York: McGraw-Hill.

Walton, F. E. (1958). "Selective distribution" of police patrol force. History, current practices, recommendations. *The Journal of Criminal Law, Criminology, and Police Science, 49*(2), 165–171.

Weisburd, D. (2008). Place-based policing. In *Ideas in American policing*. Washington D.C: Police Foundation.

Weisburd, D. (2015). The law of crime concentration and the criminology of place. *Criminology, 53*(2), 133–157.

Wilson, J. M. (2006). *Community policing in America*. New York: Taylor & Francis.

Wilson, J. Q., & Kelling, G. L. (1982). Broken windows: The police and neighborhood safety. The. *Atlantic Monthly, 249*(3), 29–38.

Wood, J. D., Sorg, E. T., Groff, E. R., Ratcliffe, J. H., & Taylor, C. J. (2014). Cops as treatment providers: Realities and ironies of police work in a foot patrol experiment. *Policing and Society, 24*(3), 362–379.

Worrall, J. L., & Schmalleger, F. (2016). *Policing* (2nd ed.). Boston: Pearson.

# The Philadelphia Experience

## The Past Rediscovered

When Michael Nutter and Charles Ramsey became Philadelphia mayor and police commissioner, respectively, they did not inherit a police department entirely unfamiliar with foot beats. Foot patrols had simply been forgotten. The Philadelphia Police Department was not immune to the desire for "professionalism" that swept police departments in the 1960s and 1970s. As we explained in the previous chapter, police departments across the world became enamored with modern communications and the police car, and foot patrol became thought of as outdated. Bruce Terris (1967: 63) noted,

> Traditionally, police officers have patrolled on foot until they saw or were notified of a crime or other occurrence needing their services. Such officers would talk to residents, and human relationships would naturally develop. Professional police departments, in contrast, have almost entirely replaced foot with motorized patrols, as the latter can cover much more area.

Even though evidence suggested that vehicle patrols were a poor replacement to police on foot, like many cities, Philadelphia embraced the sense of progress that came with the ability to react with improved speed. The standard model of policing (Weisburd and Eck 2004) and crime control became the zeitgeist. Critics who lamented the loss of police on foot were deemed sentimental for a time that never existed:

> They may claim that, in the past, when police were organized around the foot patrol, they were far more effective in dealing with crime. However, such an attitude may rest in nostalgia rather than fact. There is good reason to believe that the foot patrolman responded primarily to citizen mobilizations, he was relatively ineffective in dealing with crimes without citizen cooperation, he rarely discovered crimes in progress, and his capacity to prevent any crime was extremely limited by his restricted mobility, especially after the advent of the automobile. (Reiss 1971: 97)

© The Author(s) 2017
J.H. Ratcliffe, E.T. Sorg, *Foot Patrol*, SpringerBriefs in Criminology,
DOI 10.1007/978-3-319-65247-4_3

Philadelphia's formidable denizen, Frank Rizzo, who served as police commissioner from 1968 to 1971 and followed this with two terms as the city's mayor from 1972 to 1980, was particularly critical of foot patrols. He saw them as detracting from the efficiency and productivity that marked the new policing era (Bent 1974), saying that "The day of preventing crime is over. We have to have the ability to apprehend and this is what we do in Philadelphia" (quoted in Grimes 1971: 3). Rizzo argued that foot patrols were expensive and limited to a relatively small area, and when they were deployed, they simply caused crime displacement to an area that didn't have foot officers: "You just can't prevent it…even with communications." Even though Rizzo had whittled the number of foot patrolmen down to 100 from a force of nearly 7000 by the end of his tenure as police commissioner, he argued that "We've got more foot beat men than we had before now. Let's be practical. You put a policeman in a residential area and he walks around and says hello and shakes hands—and what good does he do? This is not policing" (Grimes 1971: 3).

Rizzo's view aside, foot patrol was the original and only method of policing when the Philadelphia Police Department was founded in 1854. For 35 years, everyone walked. Then 93 horses were added to the department in 1889, some motorcycles in 1906, and finally cars were first deployed in 1936 (Rubenstein 2015). The benefits of vehicle-bound patrols appeared clear. People who had negative opinions of the police were pleased because there was a reduction in police presence and discretion, the police could respond to the needs of the community when the community called instead of enforcing their own idiosyncratic brand of justice, and the officers were happy because they associated vehicle patrols with comfort and prestige (Moskos 2008).

Foot patrol, however, lingered in the minds of some police commanders and the community. Perhaps it was nostalgia, or perhaps it was recognition that being on foot provided something different in terms of crime prevention. As we noted in the previous chapter, foot patrol was often seen as an essential component of a community policing program in the 1980s; however, as community policing continued to develop throughout the rest of the decade, foot patrol—seen as an unfocused strategy at best—fell from favor (National Research Council 2004). Thus, with the advent of the community policing era (Klockars 1988), only sporadic efforts to maintain a presence of foot patrol officers were reported in Philadelphia. For example, a group of local residents in West Philadelphia enrolled support from a state senator to get foot patrols reintroduced to the 5700 block of Baltimore Avenue to help combat a spate of daytime robberies (Hill 1988). But these types of efforts were largely piecemeal, and the nostalgia was not universally shared. When in 1974 Mayor Frank Rizzo announced a federally funded foot patrolman program for high crime areas in North Philadelphia, complete with training that emphasized human relations, minority group cultures, and drug abuse, the announcement was met with protests (Philadelphia Tribune 1974).

The desire to professionalize policing included foot patrol but only in modest ways. For example, foot patrolmen in Philadelphia were issued with handheld radios beginning in 1968 (Philadelphia Tribune 1968). By and large, however, foot patrol was seen in Philadelphia as the lonely stepchild of the new modern era. Even with the advent of the community policing era, beat policing on foot remained (as it still does in many places) "outside the mainstream of 'real' policing and often provided only as a sop to citizens and politicians who are demanding the development of different policing styles" (Kelling and Moore 1988: 105).

While the Philadelphia Foot Patrol Experiment was radical in many ways, it was not the first foray into extensive foot beat operations in Philadelphia's recent history. In May 2002, then Mayor John Street and Police Commissioner Sylvester Johnson commenced Operation Safe Streets in an attempt to stem the tide of rising crime throughout the city (Giannetti 2007). Officers were assigned to over 200 drug-dealing corners and outside particular addresses across the city, 24 hours a day, 7 days a week. Initially, each *Safe Streets* location was assigned a pair of officers on foot, but as time wore on, locations were changed, and other forms of patrol, such as bicycle patrols, were introduced (Lawton et al. 2005). Later, roving patrols and cars were introduced to reduce costs, allowing the same officers to patrol more than one location, and police cars were "used with increasing frequency to offset the physical fatigue caused by long hours on foot" (Giannetti 2007: 26). Officers the authors have spoken with have fond memories of extensive overtime without the hassle of having to arrest people and attend court—the usual route to overtime and enhanced pay packets. Instead, they could sit on a deserted former drug-dealing corner, chat to local people or read the newspaper. Few have ever expressed any real belief that Operation Safe Streets had any meaningful or long-term effect, and the research evidence, unfortunately, supports that sentiment. While politically claimed to be a resounding success, Operation Safe Streets was found to have more modest local and temporary impacts with no meaningful broader or long-term effects (Lawton et al. 2005).

## The Philadelphia Foot Patrol Experiment

The Philadelphia Foot Patrol Experiment occurred due to a coalescence of the right people finding their way into the right positions at the right time. In 2007, Mayor Michael A. Nutter was voted into office as the 98th Mayor of the City of Philadelphia. He pledged to make public safety and violence reduction a central pillar of his administration. This had not been a clear priority of his predecessor, Mayor John F. Street, who had drawn the attention of an FBI investigation to the extent that they had placed listening bugs in his office. Street had appointed Sylvester M. Johnson to the rank of police commissioner in January 2002. Johnson was a department insider; however, Nutter sought a police commissioner from outside of the city. Nutter conducted a nationwide search, selecting Charles H. Ramsey for the position of Philadelphia's 14th police commissioner. Ramsey had previously served in the Chicago Police Department and as police chief in Washington, D.C. The appointment was regarded as a shrewd move by Nutter, with Ramsey widely respected as an innovative and thoughtful police leader.

Ramsey retained Richard Ross Jr. as his first deputy commissioner. Ross had been a deputy commissioner under Sylvester Johnson and he was keen to embrace a new direction for the department. Importantly, Ross was a strong supporter of foot patrol, having worked patrol in Philadelphia for many years (Ross would later succeed Ramsey to become Philadelphia's 15th police commissioner in 2016). Ramsey also internally promoted two new deputy commissioners as operational commanders, Thomas Wright and Kevin Bethel.

Ramsey didn't only make internal appointments, he also brought with him a couple of people from D.C., including Nola Joyce as Deputy Commissioner of Organizational Services, Strategy, and Innovation. Joyce's role was to help lead Ramsey's change management programs. She had previously worked with Ramsey in the Washington D.C. Metropolitan Police Department and prior to that as the Deputy Director of the Research and Development Division for the Chicago Police Department. In Chicago, she worked with Ramsey to develop and implement the Chicago Alternative Policing Strategy, a nationally recognized community policing model.

While Mayor Michael Nutter had made violence reduction a central campaign issue, he also ambitiously promised to reduce homicides in Philadelphia by 30–50% over the subsequent 3–5 years. On appointment, he tasked Ramsey to create a crime-fighting strategy for the police department. That strategy promised that the police department's "tactics and allocation of resources will be guided by information, intelligence, and nationally recognized best police practices. We will use accurate, current statistical data, along with human intelligence. We will develop innovative strategies to combat crime and disorder. We will constantly monitor the success of these strategies against ever changing trends and patterns" (PPD 2008: 2–3). The plan even went so far as to articulate that the Philadelphia Police Department would "support [university] faculty research designed to help us evaluate our policies, programs, training, and improve operations" (PPD 2008: 17). Ramsey and Joyce had earlier learned—through their involvement with Wes Skogan in Chicago—that researchers can play a vital role in the development of programs that are amenable to evaluation. Rather than try and cobble together an assessment of a program "after the fact," they appreciated that any impact assessment would be more robust and stronger (and thus more useful to police practitioners) if researchers were involved prior to any deployment. They later wrote:

> We learned a similar lesson with Dr. Jerry Ratcliffe of Temple University during our work with his research team on our foot patrol efforts. Our first request to Dr. Ratcliffe was if he would assess whether foot patrols made any difference after we already had them in place... Dr. Ratcliffe did make that assessment and then he offered to work with us to design a real-time evaluation the next time we implemented foot patrols. We took him up on that offer, and the result was the Philadelphia Foot Patrol Experiment. This work not only gave us needed information about foot patrol but it is now also helping to redefine how foot patrols can be used in violent areas. (Joyce et al. 2013: 360)

As part of the crime fighting strategy, an increase in foot patrols had been promised, and the department deployed a police academy graduating class on 43 foot beats for a number of weeks during the summer of 2008. While a number of the deputy commissioners were supporters of increased foot patrol, Deputy Commissioner Kevin Bethel was initially skeptical (see video at http://bit.ly/CSCS_PFPE); however, a preliminary internal evaluation suggested some potentially positive results. Therefore, Bethel reached out to Ratcliffe at Temple University.

Ratcliffe enrolled his graduate researcher, Travis Taniguchi, to help him conduct a more thorough evaluation of the foot patrol project. The difficulty that Ratcliffe and Taniguchi experienced was that they were asked to evaluate a project that had already finished. As a result, there was little documentation explaining what had occurred in the project. Worse, the foot patrol areas varied widely in size. Designed by police captains in the districts, they ranged from huge areas that were the size of the foot patrol areas in the Newark Foot Patrol Experiment (Kelling 1981) down to individual street corners (Ratcliffe and Taniguchi 2008). The resultant evaluation found some cautiously positive results; however, the design of the foot patrol project was such that a robust evaluation was not really possible. Nevertheless, the results were at least promising. When delivering the findings, Ratcliffe mentioned to Deputy Commissioner Kevin Bethel that if they ever decided to do another foot patrol project, they were welcome to contact him beforehand if the Philadelphia Police Department wanted to design a stronger and methodologically rigorous study.

One afternoon in mid-February, Bethel rang Ratcliffe and invited him to help design the next evolution of Philadelphia foot patrols. The gist of the invitation from Bethel was "we have 250 officers coming out of the academy this summer, starting in 6 weeks. Come and show us what you want to do." Ratcliffe recruited Travis Taniguchi again, along with colleagues Dr. Elizabeth Groff and Dr. Jennifer Wood. A number of graduate researchers also worked on fieldwork and other research aspects of the foot patrol evaluation.

## The Experimental Design

The Philadelphia Foot Patrol Experiment has been fully reported elsewhere (Ratcliffe et al. 2011), so what follows is a summary with some additional details not in the *Criminology* article.[1] Three years' worth of geocoded data for the locations of homicide, aggravated assault, and robberies not occurring indoors were provided by the police department and weighted so that 2008 events counted more than 2007 and 2006 crimes. These events were mapped to their nearest corner across the city, resulting in a printed map showing crime around every one of nearly 22,000 corners across Philadelphia. The corners were color coded. Red showed the top 1% of violent crime corners, while gray was used to indicate high-crime corners nearby. This was done because crime does not radiate outward evenly from high-crime corners; rather, it can be affected by local geography patterns such as how retail and

---

[1] The web page at http://bit.ly/CSCS_PFPE also describes a number of other articles related to the experiment.

commercial strips are oriented, the pattern of public transit, or where drug markets locate.

The map showed that the pattern of violence and death in Philadelphia was not evenly or randomly distributed. Crime clustered in certain neighborhoods and around certain corners. Just 1% of the nearly 22,000 corners across the city accounted for 15% of the 2008 robberies, 13% of 2008's aggravated assaults, and more than 10% of all 2008 homicides. When the distribution of the top 5% of corners for 2008 was examined, it was found they contained 39% of all robberies, 42% of aggravated assaults, and one-third of the murders.

The map was printed on the largest plotter available and then taken to police headquarters. With the potential foot patrol personnel available to cover 60 foot patrols for 16 hours a day, 5 days a week, police commanders were asked to propose 120 potential areas for foot patrol that would be subject to randomization. Deputy commissioners Kevin Bethel and Tommy Wright, the two regional operations commanders for the north and south of the city, then used a yellow marker pen to outline 129 potential foot patrol areas (a detail of this map can be seen in Fig. 1).

Of the 129, a number were either overlapping or thought to be too large for viable foot patrol beats as originally drawn. The researchers adjusted the draft areas as little as possible, but in the end some of the original foot beats were split and others were combined. The result of this process was a final list of 124 foot beats. The final areas were digitized back into a geographic information system (GIS), and a point-in-polygon GIS operation was used to reaggregate the weighted crime points from 2006 to 2008 to the new foot patrol areas. This resulted in a measure of crime in

**Fig. 1** High-crime corners (*red*) and draft potential foot patrol areas (*yellow highlight*) (Photo: Jerry Ratcliffe)

each of the potential foot beats. The four lowest crime foot beats were dropped from consideration leaving 120 potential foot patrol areas. With this preparation complete, randomization could select 60 foot patrol areas and 60 equivalent control areas.

There are many different methods of criminal justice study that can be beneficial to policy makers (Laycock and Mallender 2015); however, randomized controlled experiments are often considered to be the gold standard (Sherman 2005). Randomization has some statistical benefits but most importantly is necessary in robust experiments in order to remove the possibility of bias. Bias might creep into a place-based experiment (such as the Philadelphia Foot Patrol Experiment) if the police department were allowed to handpick the areas for foot patrol. For example, they might have selected areas where they knew the district captain was positively disposed to the use of foot patrol or where they knew the area had additional resources deployed. This *selection bias* can be countered by randomization. Randomization also guards against accidental biases that might creep into the experiment in unknown ways.

Randomized controlled experiments are rare in criminology and even rarer in policing. They often involve a blend of expedience, political will, funding, and sometimes skeptics from within the experimenters' own disciplines (Boruch 2015). Randomization was initially a difficult sell in the Philadelphia Police Department. A number of area commanders—some of whom didn't think that foot patrol would have any impact—nevertheless contended that there were specific foot beat areas that absolutely "had" to have officers posted to them. Others were (not unreasonably) concerned about the political impact on the police department when it became public knowledge that there were high-crime areas of the city that didn't have the additional patrols. The police department and Ratcliffe organized a briefing for Mayor Nutter who, on the advice of Commissioner Ramsey, gave his approval for the experiment. Ramsey's view was that the department only had the resources to police 60 areas, so why not run a rigorous experiment to find out if foot patrol could help the city?

A computer program was used to create random numbers that were assigned to each of the potential foot patrol areas in a block randomized design. Block randomized trials are a way to limit the difference between the treatment areas (that would receive foot patrol) and the control areas (Ariel and Farrington 2010). It was also beneficial politically. Block randomization avoided the (albeit slim) possibility that a totally random selection of 60 foot patrol sites might select the 60 lowest crime areas from all of the sites, leaving all of the most crime-ridden places without patrols. What this meant in practice was that the 120 potential foot patrol areas were ordered by their level of violent crime from highest to lowest. From the top two highest crime foot beats, one was randomly selected for foot patrol. Then the next pair of foot beats down the list was selected, and one was again randomly selected for foot patrol. In this way, 60 treatment and 60 control areas were selected (though one site was changed at the behest of the department from control to target area and swapped with the target area with the most similar crime rate). Fortunately, the police department had already received permission to proceed from Mayor Nutter, because the most violent foot patrol area in the city was randomly selected to be a control area. The randomization had taken place using data from 2006 to 2008, but even when the experiment started in the late spring of 2009, an examination of the violence in the 3 months before the experiment started found no difference in crime rate between the intervention sites that would have foot patrol and the control sites. The randomization was, therefore, successful in separating the treatment and control foot beats into truly comparable groups.

## *Implementing the Foot Patrols*

The Philadelphia Police Department didn't have a tradition of engaging in research prior to the Philadelphia Foot Patrol Experiment, so there was a substantial amount of skepticism and discomfort around the whole process. The department has always demonstrated a considerable degree of structural "loose coupling" where street officers can be somewhat disconnected from organizational goals, resulting in a gulf between the formal objectives and policies of the department and the actual work practices on the street (Knight 2017; Crank 2003). Some commanders were therefore initially reluctant to have their autonomy regarding assignments subverted by headquarters. When the researchers (assisted by graduate students paid on an internal grant from Temple University) accompanied officers on the foot patrols, they found that some district captains or sergeants had tacitly permitted the foot beat officers to stray from their patrol areas or given them no direction at all. One particularly belligerent captain (subsequently fired from the department for an unrelated matter) had to be specifically ordered directly from a Deputy Commissioner before the foot patrols in his area were implemented as requested. Fortunately, these teething problems were resolved fairly early in the project, and—notwithstanding every commander in the department appearing to have a firm and predetermined opinion as to the efficacy of foot patrols and the outcome—a number of the command personnel in the field were genuinely interested in the experiment and the results.

When the officers graduated from the academy, they spent about a week receiving orientation activities from a field training officer, who then accompanied the officers on the street for a few weeks. These activities could take place anywhere in the police district, so the experiment started when the officers were deployed on their own to the foot patrol areas. These areas included an average of about 15 street intersections and about a mile and a third of street length. At a walking pace of about 3 miles an hour, it was possible to cover the territory of the average foot beat area in about half an hour. Each target area was patrolled by two pairs of officers. One pair would be on patrol from 10 am to 6 pm from Tuesday to Saturday and one pair from 6 pm to 2 am on the same days. Each week the officer pairs would swap times, so they were on day shift (10 am–6 pm) 1 week and evening shift the following week. This meant that the crime hot spots were not patrolled by foot beat officers from Sunday 2 am through to Tuesday 10 am.

Officers were assigned from the academy in two phases. Phase 1 (with officers in 24 foot patrol areas) started on March 31, 2009, and continued to September. Phase 2 began on July 7, 2009, and lasted for 12 weeks, with 36 patrolled areas. Because captains were requested to keep the foot beats patrolled throughout the experiment, this theoretically provided for 57,600 hours of foot patrol activity during the initial 12 weeks of both phases (Ratcliffe et al. 2011). Of course, this was never truly achieved. Inevitably officers would be sick or called to court at no notice and replacements would be difficult to find; however, many of the district captains did their best to maintain the integrity of the experiment.

Foot patrol has never had a good reputation in Philadelphia. Prior to the arrival of Charles Ramsey, it was often viewed as a punishment posting: you did foot patrol if you screwed up in some fashion (got "jammed up"). Officers therefore wondered if they had done something to get "jammed up" and were reluctant to start their policing career on foot. This isn't just a Philadelphia phenomenon (Wilson and Kelling 1982). Writing about his year as a Baltimore cop, Harvard-trained sociologist Peter Moskos wrote "Today foot patrol is most often a form of punishment. And no police officer is ever promoted to beat cop" (Moskos 2008: 108). Both of the current authors spent their early career on foot in the East End of London (UK) and Staten Island (New York City), respectively, and can certainly understand the desire to be more mobile, comfortable, drier, and able to get to where the action is quickly. Field researchers would sometimes accompany the beat officers when vehicle-bound officers would drop by to check in on the rookies. Conversations often revolved around the foot patrol being over soon, and when it was, the rookies could get down to "real policing."

## *The Officer Experience*

The research team (Ratcliffe, Taniguchi, Groff, and Wood) and a team of hastily assembled graduate students visited all of the foot patrol teams during the experiment. This was initially tricky to organize—the Philadelphia Police Department does not have a tradition of ride-alongs with civilians accompanying officers on patrol, and no history of walk-alongs. But after overcoming some initial nerves within both the police department and Temple University[2] and subsequent to the

---

[2] Ratcliffe recalls receiving a phone call from a flustered, former University Provost who had just learned of the purchase of ballistic vests and who immediately demanded that fieldwork stop: "If you have to wear bullet-proof vests, then you can't do it." While it was pointed out that the wearing of vests was a requirement of the police department on ride-alongs (and still is), an offer to go on fieldwork *not* wearing the vests was met with stony silence. It was further pointed out that the researchers were going out with ballistic vests and armed police officers, which was a lot more protection than the university provided to students of other departments such as sociology, public health, geography and urban studies, and the medical school, all of whom were conducting fieldwork in the same areas of the city. When Ratcliffe offered to contact every other department in the university engaged in experiential learning in the city, permission to resume fieldwork soon followed!

**Fig. 2** Researchers Evan Sorg, Lallen Johnson (back to camera), and Jennifer Wood accompany foot patrol officers from the 16th District (Photo: Elizabeth R. Groff)

purchase of some new ballistic vests for the researchers, walk-alongs took place throughout the summer (Fig. 2). Each foot beat area was observed for at least 1 hour, four times throughout the experiment—twice during the day shift (10 am to 6 pm) and twice during the evening (6 pm to 2 am). Through a systematic observation protocol developed by the researchers, observers gathered data on two main themes: what were the officers doing and what they thought of their foot patrol role. The observers took some notes in the field when circumstances permitted and also recorded their impressions as soon as possible after the fieldwork. Collectively, the observations generated 90 pages of field notes (Wood et al. 2014). In addition to the fieldwork, researchers conducted 20 focus group interviews with a total of 129 foot patrol officers to learn about their perceptions and experiences during the foot patrol experiment (Wood et al. 2015).

The officers spent a lot of their time just keeping an eye on the neighborhood, and even though posted to violent crime hot spots, the officers became adept at reducing disorder. They encountered people in the direst situations that people can find themselves in within the urban milieu, including drug addicts, prostitutes, alcoholics, and people with behavioral health problems (Wood et al. 2015). They quickly developed a good sense of the "good" and "bad" people in the neighborhood. Within the foot beat areas, the officers on foot conducted many more pedestrian stops than officers in vehicles did. In fact, the rookie officers recorded over three times as many pedestrian stops as their vehicle-bound colleagues in the target areas. The foot patrol officers also performed over 1800 vehicle stops. Although on foot, the streets in much of Philadelphia are narrow and frequently one way, preventing cars from speeding too quickly. Officers could relatively easily pull cars over to the side of the road if they wished (Groff et al. 2013).

Many of the officers developed a sense of ownership over their beats and saw their role as bringing a little order to the area on behalf of the good people in the beat. Even though the personal style of the officers differed, this remained a largely common goal. Some achieved this by enforcing the law and seeking a legalistic response, while others were more informal and community oriented. For example, one officer reported buying a homeless man a haircut and a shave, and in response, he was better able to regulate the homeless man's behavior preventing him from begging in front of local shops. Some officers reflected on and acknowledged their own personal style and recognized that it differed from the two officers who worked the other shift on their beat. During focus groups, officers discussed different behaviors ranging from taking proactive action to negotiating an arrangement with a local prostitute whereby the officers and the prostitute did not work the same street at the same time (Wood et al. 2015).

We explore the experiences of the foot patrol officers in greater depth in the next chapter.


## The Limits of Beat Boundaries

As said earlier, the Philadelphia Police Department is best described as a loosely coupled department. In other words, just because an order is issued from the Roundhouse (Police Headquarters), it doesn't necessarily follow that it will be strictly adhered to in the field, or even at all. It was, therefore, no real surprise that some officers did not stick rigidly to their assigned foot beats. Officers freely acknowledged when they were outside of their assigned area. For example, one pair of officers explained that the area they had to patrol was too small; they were aware a nearby area was plagued with high crime and in need of police attention, and sometimes they followed suspicious people out of their assigned beat. Furthermore, they thought their experimentally constrained behavior had become too predictable to local drug offenders (Wood et al. 2014: 373). When a control beat was nearby, sometimes officers would inadvertently conduct activity in these control areas. We say inadvertently because the officers were not made aware of the control locations, so this was not a deliberate attempt to sabotage the experiment. Furthermore, given that control locations were also high-crime places, it is not surprising that officers might move to areas nearby perceived as problem locations. While this contamination was a modest issue for the experiment, activity in control areas accounted for less than 10% of all activity conducted by the foot patrol officers (Groff et al. 2013). We also discuss this further in the next chapter.

## *Evaluation*

When evaluating Operation Safe Streets mentioned earlier, Lawton and colleagues concluded that the operation failed to have any significant citywide impact on homicides, violent crime, or drug crimes. The evaluation of Operation Safe Streets completed by Lawton, Taylor, and Luongo (2005) had used data acquired by a local newspaper, the *Philadelphia Daily News*, and was not sanctioned by the police department (Giannetti 2007). Their access to data was limited, and attempts to gain more data were unsuccessful; however, the Philadelphia Foot Patrol Experiment had seen police and researchers work together from the start. As a result, the researchers were able to access a greater array of data to help understand the impact of the experiment.

Violent crime was measured by combining counts of criminal homicide, all robberies (except cargo theft), and most aggravated assaults. Some acts of violence were excluded from the count because it was estimated that a patrolling officer on foot could not be reasonably expected to prevent them, such as rape (which largely occurs indoors) and assaults against students when on school premises. All events in the city for the 3 months before the experiment started and the months during the experiment were identified and mapped to their respective location, be it a treatment beat, a control location, a displacement buffer area (a geographic unit that researchers use to estimate potential crime displacement, discussed further in the chapter that follows), or the remainder of the city. Fortunately, the Philadelphia Police Department has a fairly sophisticated crime mapping capability, so it is possible to map the location of about 98% of all reported crime in the city.

The statistical approach adopted is somewhat complex, involving linear regression models calculated across various percentiles of the pre-operational violence count. As these are reported in depth elsewhere (see Ratcliffe et al. 2011; corroborated in Sorg et al. 2013), only a nontechnical summary of the results is included here.

After 3 months of foot beats, the foot patrol areas were found to have suffered 23% less violent crime than their equivalent control areas. Because of some modest crime displacement to nearby areas, this violent crime reduction actually comprised of a reduction in 90 crimes in the target area that was partially offset by a 37 offense increase occurring in the areas immediately surrounding the foot beats. When the general trend in crime in the control beats and the rest of the city was considered, this translated into a reduction of 53 violent crimes that did not occur during the summer of 2009 because of the foot patrols.

It was also found that the level of crime in the beat immediately before the foot patrols commenced was an important predictor of the likelihood that the patrol area would have a reduction in violence. After controlling for the pre-experiment crime counts in the treatment and control beats in order to counter any concerns about regression to the mean, it was discovered that the effective beats were conditional on being the ones with a substantial level of crime in them before the experiment started. If a beat had six or more violent crimes in the 3 months prior to the introduction of foot patrols, then a crime reduction would likely occur as a result of the introduction of foot patrols.

The crime reduction benefits did not however last. Using multilevel growth curve models, we found (with our colleagues) that the first round of beats (that were staffed overall for longer) were less effective at keeping crime down, and the effects that were observed started to slow down the longer the experiment went on, demonstrating a type of deterrence decay (Sorg et al. 2013; Sherman 1990). Once the experiment concluded and most of the foot patrols were reassigned to different areas and districts, any benefits of the experiment disappeared.

In summary, the Philadelphia Foot Patrol Experiment demonstrated that, contrary to much of the research in the preceding decades, concise foot beats in high-crime areas can be effective in reducing crime. While some displacement is possible, and officers might not stay in their assigned areas, if a beat had a high enough level of violence prior to the deployment of the officers, significant crime reduction is possible. If they are left in place for too long, the patrols become less effective over time.

## The Philadelphia Policing Tactics Experiment

Buoyed by the success of the Philadelphia Foot Patrol Experiment (the *foot patrol* experiment) and supported by research funding from the Bureau of Justice Assistance, Temple researcher Elizabeth Groff worked with Deputy Commissioner Nola Joyce and Jerry Ratcliffe to design a more comprehensive experimental test of policing tactics for the summer of 2010. There were also sufficient funds to recruit two enterprising and enthusiastic graduate students, Evan Sorg and Cory Haberman. The Philadelphia Policing Tactics Experiment (the *tactics* experiment) was much more ambitious and used a randomized and controlled design similar to the foot patrol experiment, except this time three different policing tactics were tested: foot patrol, offender focus, and problem-oriented policing. As with the foot patrol experiment, the full details of the Philadelphia Policing Tactics Experiment have been reported elsewhere (Groff et al. 2015), and what follows is a summary, fleshed out with some details not contained in the original article, also published in *Criminology*.

Violent crime hotspots were mapped using 2009 incident data. From this process, 81 potential deployment areas were identified; however, unlike in the foot patrol study where regional commanders identified the target areas, this time the district captains for each area identified the places. By using the local area commanders, it was hoped to incorporate more local knowledge and buy-in and improve the project outcomes. The commanders, both local (captains) and regional (deputy commissioners), then chose which intervention they thought might be most applicable. After some modest adjustments, 27 areas were identified for foot beats, 27 areas for an offender focus initiative, and 27 areas for problem-oriented policing, for a total of 81 target places.

One significant difference between the *tactics* experiment and the *foot patrol* experiment was the size of the intervention areas. The district captains' inclination was to include as much area as possible, probably thinking that by doing so greater crime reductions might occur. As a result, the 81 crime hot spots for the *tactics* experiment were much larger than the *foot patrol* experiment the previous summer. The *tactics* experimental areas were about the size of 22 American football fields and much larger than the intervention sites in previous experiments such as studied in Jacksonville, Florida (Taylor et al. 2011), or Lowell, Massachusetts (Braga and Bond 2008). The *tactics* areas averaged about 3 miles of street and nearly 24 street intersections and were therefore also significantly larger than the *foot patrol* experiment areas, which were only 15 intersections and a mile-and-a-third of streets on average.

This significant difference in size is illustrated in Fig. 3 which overlays the average-sized foot patrol area from the *foot patrol* experiment with the average-sized beat area used by foot beat officers during the *tactics* experiment, against an example street network from North Philadelphia. It is clear that when this difference is transmitted across numerous beats, there is a substantial cumulative difference in the amount of area policed.

**Fig. 3** Average foot beat areas from the *foot patrol* and *tactics* experiments

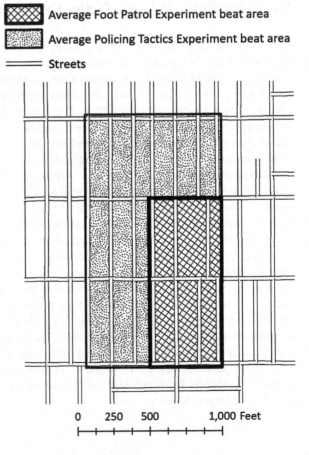

Because the police department wanted to target 60 intervention areas, it wasn't possible to identify sufficient equivalent control sites for each of the three strategies to be tested, so a stratified randomized design with an unequal randomization ratio of 3:1 was used. What this meant was that there would be 20 foot patrol areas, 20 offender focus areas, 20 problem-oriented policing areas, and 21 control sites— made up of seven areas not selected for an intervention from each of the three types of hot spot.

The offender focus sites were intelligence-led (Ratcliffe 2016), involving the identification and targeting of serious repeat offenders who either lived in the target areas or were suspected of activity in the areas. An intelligence officer from Philadelphia's Criminal Intelligence Unit prepared a brief that was made available to five-squad officers in every district that had an offender focus area. Five-squad officers are a group that is available for assignment at the discretion of the district captain and who are not normally expected to answer radio calls. They are therefore a much more fluid response team, often comprising the most motivated and dedicated patrol officers:

> According to self-report data from the OF [offender-focus] team members and patrol officers, officers made frequent contact with these prolific offenders ranging from making small talk with a known offender to serving arrest warrants for a recently committed offense. The most frequent tactic used was surveillance followed by aggressive patrol and the formation of partnerships with beat officers. OF team members in some districts used flat-screen televisions in their roll-call rooms to display photos and convey other intelligence gathered on these prolific offenders to all district personnel. (Groff et al. 2015: 34)

Officers working the problem-oriented policing (POP) sites received a one-day training session that followed the tenets of POP (Eck and Spelman 1987; Goldstein 1979, 1990). Problem-oriented policing was relatively new to the Philadelphia Police Department, who had largely paid lip service to POP in the past and had never fully embraced the notion prior to the arrival of Commissioner Ramsey. Ramsey and his new command team created a unit that specialized in POP, and they provided not only training but also personal mentorship to field personnel. Even though the experimental focus was on violence, after a quick analysis, a number of the sites changed to a focus on non-violent crime. One site lost focus on POP entirely because the district was the site of a serial rapist and killer known as "The Kensington Strangler" who was active in the latter part of 2010 until his capture in January 2011 (Hoye 2012).

## Foot Patrol During the Tactics Experiment

In the *tactics* experiment, foot patrol was implemented in a manner quite different than in the original *foot patrol* experiment. Not only were the areas much larger, they also received less treatment—what researchers call "dosage." The district captains were required by headquarters to provide a minimum beat coverage of 8 hours per day, 5 days per week, for 3 months; however, beyond this minimal stipulation, they were handed significant discretion to determine how many officers would patrol, which days and times officers would patrol, and any other operational considerations. As a result, in all but one target area, officers patrolled in pairs and worked just one shift for 5 days a week. Officers with varying years of service were used (rather than just rookies as in the *foot patrol* study), and only about half of the areas were policed by volunteers. In 11 of the areas, the officers were not volunteers but were instead assigned by the captain (note that the perspective of the officers is important here, but we defer this discussion until the next chapter).

The best results were found with the offender focus sites. While crime did increase in these areas, it was down compared to the control sites, translating to a relative decrease of 42% for all violence and a 50% decrease for violent felonies. Furthermore, there was no displacement to the surrounding streets, but instead a diffusion of crime control benefits to the areas within a couple of blocks of the offender focus areas. The POP sites had no significant findings, and while the foot patrol areas showed a very modest reduction in crime, the results were found to not be statistically significant and could have occurred by chance. Groff et al. (2015) have a more detailed discussion of what occurred with the POP and the offender focus sites, but for now we are interested in the foot patrol aspect of the *tactics* experiment and why it failed to have an impact when just one year before, in many of the same areas, it had been successful.

## How and Why Did the Experimental Results Differ?

Readers hoping foot patrol would be a "silver bullet" for the policing of urban violence will obviously be disappointed in the contradictory results from the *foot patrol* and *tactics* experiments; however, there are still important lessons from both. Possible explanations for the differential findings include area diversity and dosage.

Regarding the diversity of the area, there is a paradox first identified by David Weisburd et al. (1993) whereby experiments that had larger sample sizes (experimental areas) were less likely to report a statistically significant finding between treatment and control. This "Weisburd paradox" ran quite contrary to the conventional wisdom that larger samples made for more reliable experiments and was attributed to the reality that larger samples had higher standard deviations than the smaller samples (Sherman 2007). As a result, this reduced the statistical authority of any subsequent test because there is less statistical power to detect significant results. Statistical power is not just an issue of base rates of outcomes or sample size, but also variance. So when the Philadelphia Police Department wanted to set the number of crime hot spots that would receive a treatment at 60, inevitably there was a need to include crime hot spots that had quite a bit less crime than others. Indeed, with such a high concentration of crime in the city, as more locations got added to the potential list of treatment areas in both experiments, the number of events at each site reduced dramatically once the top sites had been included. This increased the overall diversity of the treatment areas, drastically increasing the variance and making it harder to detect significant findings.

The "hotness" of the hot spots in the *tactics* experiment may have also been a factor. The researchers used the preceding 3 years of crime data to determine areas of focus, but some of the hot spots may have seen significant recent variation in the weeks prior to the experiment. It might have been better to incorporate the most recent data if possible, though the time it takes to get operational orders distributed in the city makes that difficult. In the end, as we argue with our colleagues, "more research is needed to understand more fully and quantify the short-term temporal stability of crime hot spots to choose areas accurately for hot spot policing" (Groff et al. 2015: 44).

Dosage may have also been a significant factor. During the Philadelphia Foot Patrol Experiment, the rookie cops kept busy. The officers contributed substantially to a 64% increase in pedestrian stops, a 7% increase in vehicle stops, and a 13% increase in arrests in their treatment areas, when compared to the level of activity in those same areas in the 3 months before the beats were deployed. As an indication of comparison, in the control beats pedestrian stops hardly changed, vehicle stops declined by 13%, and arrests declined by 2%. There was clearly a substantial change in the enforcement activity in the foot patrol areas during the *foot patrol* experiment.

The *tactics* experiment differed in a few significant ways. First, there were fewer officers in each area, and they patrolled much larger crime hot spots. In the *tactics* experiment, officers were generally deployed for only one 8-hour shift (rather than two shifts as with the *foot patrol* experiment), and in a number of sites, they worked exclusively day shift, avoiding the much busier and more violent afternoon and evening periods. This, combined with the larger areas to patrol, may have meant that the officers did not manage to achieve a tipping point or threshold of dosage necessary to increase any sense of increased risk of apprehension with local offenders.

Second, the *tactics* foot patrol officers were generally veterans rather than rookies, and often were not volunteers. While we met many dedicated and enthusiastic officers who had volunteered for the duty, the non-volunteers displayed a considerable degree of skepticism and apathy towards the value of foot patrol. This appeared to be reflected in the work rate of the veteran officers: overall, pedestrian stops in the foot patrol target areas of the *tactics* experiment only increased by 5% (Ratcliffe et al. 2012). It should be borne in mind that the veteran officers had little to prove and Philadelphia does not include activity measures in any promotion considerations. The veterans might have been less enthusiastic in dealing with minor drug cases, perceived that their assignment to foot patrol was a punishment (Moskos 2008), or the veterans might have been a little less enthusiastic to report their activities formally. However, even if they had been active but paperwork-shy, the disparity between the lack of reported productivity in the *tactics* experiment and the *foot patrol* experiment's increases in pedestrian stops of 64% is remarkable.

## Where Next for Foot Patrol?

While the foot beat findings from the *foot patrol* and *tactics* experiments in Philadelphia are mixed, there is some room for optimism. Certainly the results open the door to the possibility of more study around foot patrol, a tactic that had until recently been left largely on the shelf since the Newark Foot Patrol Experiment (Kelling 1981). Some studies are starting to emerge. Recently, an experiment in Peterborough (UK) had police community support officers[3] (PCSO) patrol on foot in uniform and be as visible as possible. Each of the 34 (from a total of 72) intervention hot spots were designed to receive a minimum "dosage" of three 15 minute visits during the operational hours (3 pm to 10 pm, Tuesday to Saturday). In reality, the PSCOs made more visits (4.65 per day on average) but for less total time (overall average of 37 minutes). After 1 year, the treatment hot spots had 68 fewer crimes than would be expected relative to the control areas, translating to about a 65% greater reduction in crimes per hot spot in the treatment hot spots (Ariel et al. 2016). And in a recent nonrandomized study, Kansas City police staff and researchers worked together to identify sites for a foot patrol study (Novak et al. 2016). Rookie officers were assigned to one of four treatment areas, patrolling for two 8-hour foot patrols per day that overlapped (from 10 am to 11 pm, Tuesday to Saturday). After 90 days, panel-specific autoregressive models showed that the foot patrol implementation did not have a statistically significant impact on the number of aggravated assaults and robberies over the entire period of the project. However, the coefficients were in the right direction, and there was no evidence of displacement or any backfire effect (when things get worse). The researchers did identify an initial impact in the early phase of the foot beat implementation that was statistically significant. This might suggest the sort of treatment decay similar to the one that was observed in the Philadelphia Foot Patrol Experiment as reported in Sorg et al. (2013).

Philadelphia has also seen an increase in support for beat work. It is now standard practice that every police academy class that graduates in Philadelphia will spend a few months on foot patrol as their first assignment. District captains are increasingly seeing foot patrol as a viable deployment option when challenged with crime spikes identified in Compstat meetings ("crime briefings" as they are called in Philadelphia). And of the 117 Philadelphia Police Department officers involved in the *tactics* experiment who responded to a survey we distributed, 65% thought that a tactic designed to "Increase police visibility through expanded use of foot patrols in high-crime neighborhoods" would be either effective or very effective (Ratcliffe et al. 2012).

Dosage remains a complex and poorly understood issue. It is not the case that just throwing cops into a neighborhood appears to automatically reduce crime. Success appears to be a complex recipe of putting the right officers, doing the right

---

[3] PCSOs are civilian members of the police service, who wear a similar uniform and have fewer powers than warranted police officers. They do not carry weapons or investigate crimes, but they can issue citations for minor infractions they witness. Their role is a support function with the aim of providing reassurance and evidence of visibility.

activities, in a place that is small enough and violent enough for their activities to change the dynamic of shootings and mayhem in the area. And it should be borne in mind that our opinions on the importance on dosage here are, at present, largely conjecture. Medical science has been paying attention to issues of dosage across various treatment regimens for a while; however, in the policing field, this interest is still embryonic. As Sherman has pointed out, "there is no independent evidence of how much dosage is 'enough' for good results in problem-oriented policing or any evidence that dosage levels matter more than the content of the strategy" (Sherman 2007: 311).

Whatever the sufficient dosage is, it requires the collaboration and cooperation of officers who actually walk the beat. The next chapter unpacks the experiences of officers on foot patrol and explores their perspectives on walking a beat and the work they are asked to do.

# References

Ariel, B., & Farrington, D. P. (2010). Randomized block designs. In D. Weisburd & A. Piquero (Eds.), *Handbook of quantitative criminology* (pp. 437–454). New York: Springer.

Ariel, B., Weinborn, C., & Sherman, L. W. (2016). "Soft" policing at hot spots—Do police community support officers work? A randomized controlled trial. *Journal of Experimental Criminology, 12*(3), 277–317.

Bent, A. E. (1974). *The politics of law enforcement: Conflict and power in urban communities*. Lexington, MA: Lexington books.

Boruch, R. (2015). Street walking: Randomized controlled trials in criminology, education, and elsewhere. *Journal of Experimental Criminology, 11*(4), 485–499.

Braga, A. A., & Bond, B. J. (2008). Policing crime and disorder hot spots: A randomized controlled trial. *Criminology, 46*(3), 577–607.

Crank, J. P. (2003). Institutional theory of police: A review of the state of the art. *Policing: An International Journal of Police Strategies & Management, 26*(2), 186–207.

Eck, J. E., & Spelman, W. (1987). *Problem solving: Problem-oriented policing in Newport News*. Washington, D.C.: Police Executive Research Forum.

Giannetti, W. J. (2007). What is operation safe streets? *IALEIA Journal, 17*(1), 22–32.

Goldstein, H. (1979). Improving policing: A problem-oriented approach. *Crime and Delinquency, 25*(2), 236–258.

Goldstein, H. (1990). *Problem-oriented policing*. New York: McGraw-Hill.

Grimes, S. (1971). *Foot patrolmen losing out to red cars*. Philadelphia Bulletin. Feb 4th.

Groff, E. R., Johnson, L., Ratcliffe, J. H., & Wood, J. D. (2013). Exploring the relationship between foot and car patrol in violent crime areas. *Policing: An International Journal of Police Strategies and Management, 36*(1), 119–139.

Groff, E. R., Ratcliffe, J. H., Haberman, C., Sorg, E., Joyce, N., & Taylor, R. B. (2015). Does what police do at hot spots matter? The Philadelphia policing tactics experiment. *Criminology, 51*(1), 23–53.

Hill, T. S. (1988). *Foot patrolmen doing the job in West Philadelphia*. Philadelphia Tribune. Mar 15.

Hoye, S. (2012). Accused 'Kensington Strangler' convicted in Philadelphia, given three life sentences. http://edition.cnn.com/2012/08/16/us/pennsylvania-strangler-conviction/ CNN online. Accessed 1 June 2017.

Joyce, N. M., Ramsey, C. H., & Stewart, J. K. (2013). Commentary on smart policing. *Police Quarterly, 16*(3), 358–368.

Kelling, G. L. (1981). *The Newark foot patrol experiment*. Washington, D.C.: Police Foundation.

Kelling, G. L., & Moore, M. H. (1988). The evolving strategy of policing. *Perspectives on Policing, 4*(November), 1–15.

Klockars, C. B. (1988). The rhetoric of community policing. In J. R. Greene & S. D. Mastrofski (Eds.), *Community policing: Rhetoric of reality* (pp. 239–258). New York: Praeger.

Knight, G. M. (2017). The impact of loose coupling on police effectiveness. *Australian and New Zealand Journal of Criminology, 50*(2), 269–281.

Lawton, B. A., Taylor, R. B., & Luongo, A. J. (2005). Police officers on drug corners in Philadelphia, drug crime, and violent crime: Intended, diffusion, and displacement impacts. *Justice Quarterly, 22*(4), 427–451.

Laycock, G., & Mallender, J. (2015). Right method, right price: The economic value and associated risks of experimentation. *Journal of Experimental Criminology, 11*(4), 653–668.

Moskos, P. (2008). *Cop in the hood: My year policing Baltimore's Eastern District*. Princeton: Princeton University Press.

National Research Council. (2004). *Fairness and effectiveness in policing: The evidence* (p. 413). Washington, D.C.: Committee to Law and Justice, Division of Behavioral and Social Sciences and Education.

Novak, K. J., Fox, A. M., Carr, C. M., & Spade, D. A. (2016). The efficacy of foot patrol in violent places. *Journal of Experimental Criminology, 12*(3), 465–475.

Philadelphia Tribune. (1968, January 27). Foot patrolmen will get Walkie-Talkies. *Philadelphia Tribune*.

Philadelphia Tribune. (1974, March 23). Foot patrolmen return to North Philadelphia. *Philadelphia Tribune*.

PPD. (2008). *Philadelphia police Department's crime fighting strategy* (p. 21). Philadelphia: Philadelphia Police Department.

Ratcliffe, J. H. (2016). *Intelligence-led policing* (2nd ed.). Abingdon: Routledge.

Ratcliffe, J. H., & Taniguchi, T. (2008). *A preliminary evaluation of the crime reduction effectiveness of the PPD footbeat program* (p. 17). Philadelphia: Temple University (Unpublished).

Ratcliffe, J. H., Taniguchi, T., Groff, E. R., & Wood, J. D. (2011). The Philadelphia Foot Patrol Experiment: A randomized controlled trial of police patrol effectiveness in violent crime hotspots. *Criminology, 49*(3), 795–831.

Ratcliffe, J. H., Groff, E. R., Haberman, C. P., & Sorg, E. T. (2012). *Smart policing initiative final report (Unpublished)* (p. 92). Washington DC: Bureau of Justice Assistance.

Reiss, A. J., Jr. (1971). *The police and the public*. New Haven: Yale University Press.

Rubenstein, D. (2015). *Born to walk*. Toronto: ECW Press.

Sherman, L. W. (1990). Police crackdowns: Initial and residual deterrence. In M. Tonry & N. Morris (Eds.), *Crime and justice: An annual review of research* (Vol. 12, pp. 1–48). Chicago: University of Chicago Press.

Sherman, L. W. (2005). The use and usefulness of criminology, 1751-2005: Enlightened justice and its failures. *Annals of the American Academy of Political and Social Science, 600*, 115–135.

Sherman, L. W. (2007). The power few: Experimental criminology and the reduction of harm. *Journal of Experimental Criminology, 3*(4), 299–321.

Sorg, E. T., Haberman, C. P., Ratcliffe, J. H., & Groff, E. R. (2013). Foot patrol in violent crime hot spots: Longitudinal impacts of deterrence and post-treatment effects of displacement. *Criminology, 51*(1), 65–101.

Taylor, B., Koper, C. S., & Woods, D. J. (2011). A randomized controlled trial of different policing strategies at hot spots of violent crime. *Journal of Experimental Criminology, 7*(2), 149–181.

Terris, B. J. (1967). The role of the police. *Annals, American Academy of Political and Social Science, 374*(1), 58–69.

Weisburd, D., & Eck, J. (2004). What can police do to reduce crime, disorder, and fear? *The Annals of the American Academy of Political and Social Science, 593*(1), 43–65.

Weisburd, D., Petrosino, A., & Mason, G. (1993). Design sensitivity in criminal justice experiments. In M. Tonry (Ed.), *Crime and justice: A review of research* (Vol. 17, pp. 337–379). Chicago: University of Chicago.

Wilson, J. Q., & Kelling, G. L. (1982). Broken windows: The police and neighborhood safety. The. *Atlantic Monthly, 249*(3), 29–38.

Wood, J. D., Sorg, E. T., Groff, E. R., Ratcliffe, J. H., & Taylor, C. J. (2014). Cops as treatment providers: Realities and ironies of police work in a foot patrol experiment. *Policing and Society, 24*(3), 362–379.

Wood, J. D., Taylor, C. J., Groff, E. R., & Ratcliffe, J. H. (2015). Aligning policing and public health promotion: Insights from the world of foot patrol. *Police Practice and Research, 16*(3), 211–223.

# The Foot Beat Experience

*A good police officer is never wet, cold, hot, or hungry.*

The origins of the above phrase are unknown, but it has been a police mantra for decades. Unfortunately, the idea that patrol officers, who work outside on every day of every season in every climate, could avoid heat, cold, or precipitation is folklore. This is especially true for police on foot patrol. Officers on foot don't have the luxury of a climate-controlled patrol car and the protection from the elements that it affords. Patrolling on foot can be unpleasant at times, as both of us writing this book have regularly experienced. We've been there! It is not surprising, then, that foot patrol work is seen by many officers as something to be avoided.

While in a few departments, it is a sought-after chance to escape the grind of constant radio calls, in others a posting to a foot patrol is used as an informal punishment. And in many places, as with our research findings in Philadelphia, foot patrolling is not always thought of as real police work. This is not, however, a universal perspective. For example, in a recent conversation with one of the authors, D. Kim Rossmo (research professor at Texas State University and a former Detective Inspector with the Vancouver Police Department) revealed that within the Vancouver Police Department being assigned to a beat team, which performed foot patrols, is considered an elite position. Officers welcomed the freedom to escape the radio and engage in preventative and community work. We therefore caution that our findings may not automatically apply to agencies outside of Philadelphia. Through our experience working with numerous police departments in the United States, however, we are confident that many of the sentiments expressed in the pages that follow apply to many law enforcement agencies.

What is required to get officers to engage with the work and do it well—and what does good foot patrol work look like? How do we get officers to buy into the idea that foot patrol has value, as is the case in Vancouver? How do we ensure that the evaluation of officers' work aligns with the instrumental outcomes that foot patrol programs seek to achieve? And how do we get them to adhere to principles and

© The Author(s) 2017
J.H. Ratcliffe, E.T. Sorg, *Foot Patrol*, SpringerBriefs in Criminology,
DOI 10.1007/978-3-319-65247-4_4

theories that have driven effective place-based policing generally (Mastrofski et al. 2010) and foot patrols at hot spots specifically (Ratcliffe et al. 2011)?

These are not just philosophical or academic questions. Understanding the intricacies of police foot patrols can mean the difference between a successful or an unsuccessful program, a satisfied or unsatisfied rank-and-file workforce, and a community that works with police as opposed to being indifferent to their efforts. Listening to the experience of officers that do the work therefore has immense value, as it could offer important nuances to policies that ultimately determine success or failure.

Putting aside the perception of unpleasantness that comes with the thought of a foot post, our work in Philadelphia revealed that foot patrolling has organizational complexities that officers can struggle to negotiate. Officers faced internal (departmental) and external (community) pressures, and these pressures oftentimes conflicted not just with each other but also with traditional police cultural values. In many cases, orders coming from the top of the police organization did not translate well into practice on the street. To navigate these conflicts, we found officers would bend rules, negotiate around various constraints placed upon them, and police their assigned territories with a great deal of autonomy. We learned that Egon Bittner's (1967) conceptualization of policing as a "craft" still resonates today, as officers used the various legal and nonlegal tools available to them to police their beats, using methods that were dependent upon both situational and spatial exigencies.

How, then, can police executives effectively manage their personnel and ensure adherence to the organizational mission while also providing the autonomy that appears vital to properly addressing the idiosyncrasies of each post and its varied criminogenic circumstances? Is traditional top-down organizational control more appropriate than a decentralized management structure that has been emphasized under community policing models? Can foot patrols properly function under the former, and can crime reductions via hotspot foot patrols be realized while emphasizing the latter? Or is it, as we suspect, that police foot patrols can straddle these two paradigms and play an important role in "reinventing American policing," a role that scholars believe the twenty-first century police agencies must embrace (Lum and Nagin 2017)? In order to make our case, we must dig deeper into the minutia of what it is like to patrol on foot. We do that here.

In the process, we tell the story of how officers navigated the world of foot patrol in a rather traditional "professional" police organization, and under restrictive experimental conditions, and negotiated these sometimes conflicting pressures and mismatched priorities. Our goal here is to give a voice to the officers who were kind enough to let us share in the experience of patrolling on foot in Philadelphia's most violent neighborhoods. The nuanced accounts of their experiences that we captured during our experiments offer police leaders interested in adopting similar foot patrol programs guidance for program planning and execution, what should be avoided, and what should be emphasized. As we have argued with our colleagues elsewhere:

> Our data underscore the importance of listening to what line officers have to say about the realities of police work…Line officers may have clear directives from management about the desired instrumental outcome of the intervention (reduction in violence or other crimes), but they know that other ends must be considered, and other means negotiated. (Wood et al. 2014:374)

We will explore several themes that have emerged during the analysis of the vast quantitative and qualitative data that were collected during our experiments. These data include field notes, interview transcripts, and various forms of spatial data, such as crime, disorder, and officer activity records. We believe our experiments are unique in that our analyses did not end with experimental evaluations. Rather, along with our colleagues, we have conducted and published ten separate analyses that have explored foot patrol from a number of vantage points (Ratcliffe et al. 2011, 2015; Groff et al. 2013, 2015; Wood et al. 2014, 2015; Sorg et al. 2013, 2014, 2016; Haberman et al. 2016). Here, we bring together what we learned and tell the story of what it is like to walk Philadelphia's most dangerous hot spots.

## What Is Real Police Work?

As policing scholars, it is not uncommon for us to arrive at some social affair, reveal the types of work that we do and did, and to subsequently be subjected to lay ramblings about how police can best go about their work. Everyone has an opinion about policing. Unfortunately, much of what we hear has little basis in reality. It is frequently grounded in the misplaced notion that the majority of police work involves crime fighting—rushing to the scene of ubiquitous violent crimes, chasing bad guys, and making arrests. Even in high-crime jurisdictions, this is simply not the case. Unfortunately, television shows such as *Cops* and *Law and Order* have done much to sensationalize this singular narrow role of police work and to cement the idea of police as first and foremost crime fighters. In turn, the police themselves look to embody the image of the crime fighter, and this hinders many agencies' ability to adopt innovative and evidence-based strategies.

Police were not passively ascribed the crime fighter label. Police organizations, training, and culture do much to reinforce it. For example, police are bestowed honors and awards for making a good pinch, but few departments reward good community work or problem-solving activities that prevent crime from happening in the first place. At the end of the month, officers submit their activity reports that capture arrests, citations issued, and stop-and-frisk tallies to gauge their effectiveness, but they are not judged by their community contacts nor are "problems solved" an easy activity to quantify. Police training emphasizes procedures but usually does a poor job of training officers on problem solving or conveying to new officers the empirical evidence relating to what does and does not work in crime and problem reduction. New officers quickly learn that a "cop's cop" is valued because he or she is someone who backs others up and has a reputation for making big arrests. Combined, these truths reinforce the traditional conceptualization of police as crime fighters, and police officers are often eager to embrace it.

This point was particularly salient during our time walking with rookies fresh from the academy. During the Philadelphia Foot Patrol Experiment, it was not uncommon to hear that officers did not view their foot patrol duties as real police work. After performing a field observation, for example, a graduate student field worker recorded the following statement and officer quote:

> They [the officers] were happy to hear that they would be off foot beats soon, and were extremely excited for new experiences. "I'm excited to be doing, you know, like real police work: going to jobs, making good pinches, in a car. That's what I see as real police work."

Officers did not see the foot patrols, which elicited an impressive 23% reduction in violent crime during the summer of 2009, as something worthwhile. Rather, their perception was that reactive work such as making arrests and rapidly responding to 911 calls had more value. Yet as we discussed in previous chapters, these tenets of the standard model of policing have little impact on crime. This misconception, even among officers who had just months earlier graduated the police academy, is in part a consequence of the crime-fighter image. At least for the pair of officers who were observed prior to penning the diary entry below, the results of the Philadelphia Foot Patrol Experiment were counter to their expectation:

> I asked if this experiment would be beneficial to them or to police departments and they agreed that it may be helpful in assessing whether foot beats are effective. They were confident, however, that it would show that they are not. "Compared to what we could be doing in a car, these foot beats are a waste." The way they explained it said to me that they saw police work as responding to calls for service and arresting bad guys.

The nature of the 911 system undoubtedly plays a role in cementing the perception that prompt response to 911 calls is the most important job that an officer engages in. In busy police districts, the sheer volume of 911 calls can force a patrol squad into backlog if they are unable to keep up. Academics can tell police that they need to be proactive and solve problems, but in many high-crime areas, this simply isn't realistic within the constraints of a system that emphasizes another metric. Emphasis is placed on efficiently handling and disposing of calls to avoid backlog for the next tour. This is work that must be done—the public expects the police to arrive when they call them. Since 911 responses consume the greatest amount of a patrol officer's time, it is no wonder that many police see this as real police work and the activity that should be prioritized. As foot patrol officers that we accompanied listened to their colleagues struggle to keep up with calls for service, they questioned the utility of their assignments and wondered why they were not in cars helping out. Consider the following diary entry from an observer in South Philadelphia:

> They thought cars were a much better way to police, because of the ability to move around and deal with more problems. This lack of mobility was one of the things they spoke of the most. They said it was frustrating to hear calls for help from other officers, and they were unable to assist or respond. They said this was true for radio calls, as sometimes they are just too far away to respond, but close enough that if they had a car they could get to them sooner. They said that their district was so understaffed that it made no sense to have them on foot beats.

This perception of foot patrol not being real police work is one of the most significant impediments to adopting a proactive foot patrol program. And the officers performing the foot duty were not the only ones who thought that foot beats were a waste of time. Our conversations with seasoned police commanders before and after our experiments revealed that many were skeptical of foot patrol's value. Commanders leading districts that lacked sufficient personnel resources believed that their officers could be better utilized in cars to help respond to 911 calls. To be fair, it is almost impossible to find a police commander in any jurisdiction in just about any country that feels they are appropriately resourced. But the issue is more one of how best to use a finite resource. Academic research has had little success infiltrating police decision-making, and there are still too few innovative leaders that accept the idea that policing should be driven by empirical evidence about what works.

As Lum (2009) laid out in her contribution to *Ideas in American Policing*, the adoption of evidence-based policing that Sherman (1998) articulated about a decade earlier has not changed the way that a meaningful number of police agencies operate. Lum (2009: 3) noted that:

> From the perspective of a practitioner, it is not surprising that the factors that go into the vast majority of police decisions on the street and at the level of high command are not evidence or science based. The daily activities, strategies, and tactics of the police are driven not by analytic intelligence, crime analysis and maps, systematically collected observations, or performance measures related to crime prevention outcomes but instead by a procedural reaction to 911 calls.

Nevertheless, we share in Lum's (2009) ultimate optimism that the infrastructure for change has been built over the last few decades and that adjustments to the status quo may allow for widespread adoption of proactive, hotspot foot patrols in departments wishing to incorporate them.

We should be clear that we are not criticizing police or the cultural norms by which they work. As we have made clear elsewhere, police are not "passive recipients of culture" (Wood et al. 2014: 372). We believe that heroic cops should undoubtedly be recognized and offered commendations for saving a life or taking a prolific or dangerous criminal off the street. Our concern here lies in a historical unwillingness to embrace different ideas. There is increasing evidence that foot patrol fulfills many key roles asked of police departments, yet the myth of a walking beat not being real policing harms enthusiasm to take on the role, to supervise and employ foot beats effectively, and to maximize the benefits of this most fundamental policing function. Of course, not all officers hold such views; nevertheless, a change in attitude is deserved, and it has to start at the police academy and continue beyond field training, actively supported by leadership.

## What Did Foot Patrol Officers Do?

What should police officers do on foot? On hearing we were writing this book on police foot patrols, some people asked how we could possibly fill an entire volume on the topic. At face value what officers should do appears obvious, but for many officers that we spoke to, there was no easy answer or way to explain the subtleties of dealing with the intricacies of a high-crime neighborhood. The criminogenic circumstances that officers are presented with when assigned to a hotspot foot post tend to exhibit considerable diversity. There is no one-size-fits-all solution that is appropriate for all places, and this is perhaps why many of the foot patrol officers that were a part of our experiments were told to just go out on foot and "police." Few reported being given a mission by their commanders. As a result, the specific tactics that officers engaged in depended upon the officers' perceptions of the characteristics of the crime or disorder problem that faced them, combined with the characters of the officers and their take on what would be the most effective response. This resulted in a great deal of heterogeneity in the activities that officers undertook during our experiments, even when policing in superficially similar circumstances.

In this sense, Bittner's (1967) depiction of skid-row policing paralleled our own observations of police patrolling on foot in Philadelphia's most violent neighborhoods over 30 years later. Policing, it seems, is still a craft that officers sharpen as they gain experience in dealing with the various "situational exigencies" that they encounter (Bittner 1967: 701). Decisions on how to police generally, and how to handle specific situations, oftentimes depended upon their understanding of the communities that officers served. As was the case in Bittner's observation of policing on skid row, officers became more effective at controlling problem behaviors as they got to know the communities in which they worked—who was good, who was bad, who belonged, and who did not. This was highlighted in a field diary entry from West Philadelphia recorded in August of 2009:

> One officer believed that "[o]ne positive [aspect] about walking a foot beat is that you become familiar with the people of the neighborhood." They thought they used this to their advantage because they can easily tell who is out of place and who does not belong. They reported that when they first arrived they thought everyone was "up to no good" but now that they have been around for a bit, they are able to differentiate between the good and bad. A known drug dealer was walking down the street and the officers yelled to him, "Go home Anton," and he looked back and continued walking away.

Here, the officers are exerting what Herbert (1997) referred to as spatial control, and it was facilitated by their in-depth understanding of their patrol areas. Even though the officers took no official police action in this case, they were nevertheless staking claim to the foot beats that they were assigned: "Asking someone to 'move along' symbolizes an officer's claim to space or place" (Wood et al. 2014: 366). This was an informal strategy that many officers relied upon to keep order and dissuade criminal behavior during their shifts. Even rookie officers working during the Philadelphia Foot Patrol Experiment quickly learned that their badge and power to enforce the criminal law allowed them to informally regulate their beats without having to take any official police action. These informal actions included simply being present at a place. For example, at the end of July 2009 in South Philadelphia, one field researcher noted that, "They [the officers] have noticed that crowds now disperse at the sight of the officers, and the officers seem to be appreciative of this respect." Simply standing on a corner was a deterrent strategy that many officers used to disrupt activities like drug sales, loitering crowds, or prostitution.

Although officers used many informal means to police their beats, their status as law enforcement officers provided them legal mechanisms to deploy during the course of their work. The ability to stop, question, frisk, detain, cite, and arrest members of the public is not only central to officers' ability to informally regulate people and places; these various means were also seen as important tools for addressing disorder, preventing crime (even if for a time), and holding violators of the criminal law accountable. During our observations, they frequently engaged their legal mandate. But many officers, even rookie officers, recognized the limitations of these formal actions. Officers wrestled with whether an emphasis on community-oriented policing might be "not rough enough," and whether cracking down and a heavy emphasis on law enforcement was "too rough," as Bittner (1967: 701) put it. Consider the following interaction that a field researcher had with a pair of officers patrolling a housing project in South Philadelphia:

> These officers took a very different approach from the other pair of officers that shared the housing project beat. They were very friendly, much less enforcement and much more community oriented. Though the officers agreed that when action was necessary, they would take it, they stressed that there is no need to be harsh on the residents of the neighborhood because they are, for the most part, 'good people.' They acknowledged that their counterparts they share a beat with were very enforcement oriented, and that the two pairs of beat officers balanced each other out. They did express disagreement with their counterparts in the particular policing style, but conceded that they did not expressly know if theirs was better.

When probed about whether focusing on community-centered activities or enforcement of the criminal law was more effective, these officers were unsure. And perhaps this is to be expected. Academia has, to date, been unable to definitively provide an answer either. In an academic sense, this is illustrative of the "black box" (Sherman and Strang 2004) problem that is inherent in experimental research. Although we were able to discern that foot patrols at hot spots reduced crime in Philadelphia during our first experiment by 23% relative to controls, we cannot discern from any of our analyses what exact mechanisms were responsible for those declines. Indeed, enforcement activities and positive community interactions were both commonly employed and recurring themes in our qualitative data. On the one hand, officers recognize the importance of positively interacting with community residents, and in this field diary entry captured in July of 2009, especially children:

> These officers appear to have developed a rapport with the neighborhood residents, and stopped to talk to many of them, and even spent time playing football with some of the kids. The kids were happy to play with the officers, and they threw passes for about 15 minutes before walking along. It was nice to see such an interaction, and the parents and older residents that watched along with me were smiling and seemed to be pleased as well. As we walked, an older gentleman stopped and said, "That's not something you see every day,

cops playing with kids." The officers laughed and said it was their pleasure. I asked them if this was something they did on a regular basis, and they said that they try to interact with children as much as possible. While they found that most were receptive to them, some kids even as young as 10 years old already have the mentality that cops are bad and either ignore them or walk away from them.

On the other hand, some officers believed that they could be most effective if they adopted a more "zero-tolerance" approach and emphasized positive community contacts to a lesser extent:

These officers stated that they tended to focus on fighting crime. They did take an obviously enforcement based approach, and although they did not take any formal police action, they gave the impression of being stringent and enforcing the rules. They made little contact with the residents of the neighborhood, and there seemed to be uneasiness in the relationship between the officers and the residents. Some residents turned as the officers approached and some stared from their porches. One person asked who I was, and the officers responded with, "He's with us," and we continued walking.

Another set of officers responded to a question regarding which tactic is more appropriate with the following response:

I asked if community contact was as important as fighting crime, and they thought that their main objective was to fight crime and respond to jobs, and that community relationships should be secondary.

A majority, though, employed a combination of both, used their discretion when appropriate, and saw the obvious benefits of both policing styles:

They used their discretion to not write a male drinking a beer a summons despite his doing so. They ran him through central for warrants with negative results. They reasoned that they would rather start off having a good relationship with people, and that a warning suffices for the first encounter. If they were to run into him again, they would then bring him into the station and write him a summons. Since he had no warrants he got a free pass since it was his first run in with them, and since he lived nearby. Had he been an outsider, they stated, he would have been brought in. They want to have a good relationship and be trusted by the residents of the housing development, but also want to send the message to outsiders that criminal activity inside the boundaries of the project will not be tolerated.

With few exceptions, officers were cognizant of the "value pluralism" (Thacher 2001: 388) that was inherent in their work. It was important to them that the communities that they policed were satisfied, that they appreciated the officers' efforts, and that they saw the officers as allies in addressing the crime and disorder problems that were present. At the same time, the officers had a job to do, and this included enforcing the criminal law and getting justice for crime victims through arresting and prosecuting law violators. It might not be an unreasonable conclusion that both community-oriented and enforcement-based foot patrols likely have a role to play, and we discuss tasking officers in more depth in the chapter that follows.

## Harm Reduction and Harm-Focused Policing

Although crime rates have been on the decline since at least the 1990s, the workload of police has hardly leveled off (Ratcliffe 2015), and there remains, in many large urban departments a "demand gap" between what the police are tasked with handling and the personnel resources available to these agencies (Ratcliffe 2016). Although many agencies remain squarely focused on reducing serious forms of violence, there is a growing recognition that police are tasked with dealing with many harmful behaviors that do not rise to what would be considered a serious crime. Examples include drug overdoses and traffic accidents. While more in the realm of public health, nevertheless these become the responsibility of police to handle. As a result, many police leaders have come to the realization that focusing solely on violent crime is too limiting for twenty-first century policing (Ratcliffe 2016). Progressive departments have therefore become focused on addressing various sources of community harm, be they crime, disorder, behavioral health, or other harmful community conditions such as addiction or homelessness.

At the conclusion of the Philadelphia Foot Patrol Experiment, our colleague Jennifer Wood conducted focus groups with officers involved in the experiment. Her line of research explored themes related to how officers approached not only disorder and crime but also public health-related issues, such as addicted or mentally ill individuals (Wood et al. 2015). An advocate of harm-focused policing, one of us has argued that "Harm-focused policing aims to inform policing priorities by weighing the harms of criminality together with data from beyond crime and disorder, in order to focus police resources in furtherance of both crime and harm reduction" (Ratcliffe 2015: 3). We do not intend to debate the merits of such an approach here but rather to examine the potential impediments to implementing such an approach in police departments that emphasize the crime-fighting activities discussed above.

Through her focus groups, our colleague Jennifer Wood identified a tension between how police have come to view issues surrounding public health harms such as addiction and what police (as crime fighters) see as the proper method of handling individuals who, by the very nature of their status, are at odds with the law. For example, Wood et al. (2015) noted that:

> It was challenging for officers to conceive of addicted drug users as vulnerable people at higher risks of morbidity and mortality. As has always been the police mandate, officers were more concerned about protecting the public from the health risks of the criminal behavior associated with drug markets. In public health terms, the public protection mandate of the police would over-ride the principles of individual harm reduction. This was especially the case for injection drug and crack cocaine users who were seen by some officers as having no desire to abstain from drugs in the long term. As part of this belief, methadone programs simply served to substitute one drug for another. Methadone, an officer argued, simply 'gets them high at a lower dose' (FG 9). Another officer said, '[p]eople will claim that they've been clean because they've been going to methadone, but it's the same thing with the same effects; people are still 'zombies'.

Perhaps it was a reflection of their newness, but the rookie officers were skeptical of programs intended to address harms not necessarily related to crime, such as the methadone programs noted above or in other instances needle exchange programs. Officers saw such efforts not as a means of reducing harm but as providing criminals with opportunities to acquire the needles used to inject drugs. Regardless, many officers believed that drug users were a hopeless population, and one not even deserving of police attention. For example, one officer quoted by Wood and colleagues (Wood et al. 2015) stated that they would rather focus on drug suppliers than dealers because drug users are "done anyway." In other words, they were not worth saving because they had given up on their lives as a result of their addiction. At least for the officers quoted above, they did not see their role as a social service provider but rather as a crime fighter.

How could harm be more incorporated into foot patrol work? Harm-focused policing could be developed in a myriad of ways that would benefit a department and the community. For example, foot patrol areas could be selected on the basis of harm scores rather than just crime—an approach that has been shown to demonstrate subtle differences in hotspot areas (Ratcliffe 2015). Incorporating drug overdoses and other community harms may also affect the selection of target places for intervention. Officers could be tasked and their productivity assessed on metrics that reflect the harms in an area. This might be a mechanism to encourage officers to engage with problem-oriented policing of community harms. Violence fluctuates in and around drug markets depending on the characteristics of the market participants (Johnson 2016), but violence is only one (albeit important) harm. Overdoses are hugely harmful to the public as well. Prioritizing attention to drug markets based on a combination of overdoses and violence may be beneficial.

Harm-focused policing recognizes the different perspectives that community and police leaders may have with regard to what is important in policing. Indeed police administrators have long recognized the ways in which foot patrols could benefit the police-community relationship. They were commonplace in many cities that moved to a community policing model in the 1980s and 1990s. Recent calls to "reimagine" policing in the twenty-first century likewise suggest that police effectiveness should be judged by crimes prevented and by how the community views their police and the tactics that they employ (Lum and Nagin 2017). In Philadelphia, foot patrols were utilized in ways that likely influenced both outcomes in positive ways. But we also found that foot patrols that emphasize developing a rapport with the community allowed officers to develop knowledge and intelligence that ultimately resulted in information that was actionable. It was clear that in some cases, had officers not engaged the community or, worse, alienated the community with overly aggressive tactics, this knowledge would not have been gleaned. For example, one pair of officers relayed that, "they do get criminal intelligence from residents of the neighborhood, such as being told that there was a chop shop on a corner in their beat, which they were able to shut down."

Bittner (1967: 715) referred to this as an "immensely detailed knowledge." Their ability to generate this intelligence and to develop a more nuanced understanding of neighborhood dynamics was not lost on the officers who participated in our studies.

As we noted with our colleagues previously, "The pace of foot patrol is different from that of motor patrol or other specialized units...Officers have the opportunity to 'take in' the rhythm and flow of the streets, and the dynamics that constitute its social relations" (Wood et al. 2014: 366). As a result of this, it was not uncommon for officers to suggest that foot patrols were superior in this sense. As the experiment was coming to a close, a field researcher asked a pair of officers if they should be assigned to the same sector when they are put in regular patrol squads and moved to cars. The reasoning behind their affirmative response is captured in the diary entry below:

> I asked if they wanted to work in the same sector that they walked in [when they are put in cars], and they said it would probably be the smartest idea. "We know these people and can tell the good from the bad, we should totally work this area." I asked if they knew more than the guys that have been patrolling in the car, and they believed they did. "The one good thing about foot patrol is that you learn about the neighborhood—the guys in cars never get out so they don't know half of what we know." They thought they could use this to their benefit. "Some people trust us here so we may be able to get information from them if something comes up." I asked if this meant that they thought foot patrolling was beneficial, and they said that it was in ways.

Police foot patrols are versatile enough that we saw them utilized as a means of cracking down at hot spots of crime, a tool to increase trust and improve police-community relations and an instrument for gathering intelligence. Many officers were acutely aware of the community harms in their beats and tried to do what they could to mitigate the problems in the area. During many of our conversations with foot patrol officers, it was clear that they used their judgment in deciding which tactic to employ in order to achieve whatever the desired end was. Many believed that foot patrols were better suited to achieve these goals even if they were not thrilled with the idea of performing them. But in addition to situational judgments, the actions that officers undertook were likewise influenced by the management structure of the Philadelphia Police Department and what their commanders expected of them. Policing is not carried out in a vacuum, and we learned that managerial expectations, or perceived expectations in the absence of explicit instructions, frequently shaped the decision-making of officers out in the field.

## The Conundrum of Performance Evaluations

### *Balancing Community Work with Enforcement Actions*

Officers recognized that they are judged by the outputs that they produce. At Compstat meetings around the country, district-level police commanders demonstrate that they are "doing something" to address crime by presenting evidence of outputs such as activities like stop and frisk and arrests that their officers performed. In Philadelphia, these activities are geolocated digitally, mapped, and displayed in "the war room" during crime briefings (the Philadelphia Police Department equivalent of a Compstat meeting). At crime briefings, executive officers interrogate district-level supervisors about the crime problems and the concomitant police activity levels. We have witnessed commanders show up to a crime briefing with little activity to show in the face of a rising crime problem have a decidedly uncomfortable time as their command ability and capacity to motivate their officers was called into question. In Philadelphia, as with many other traditional police agencies, Compstat has become a game of "whack-a-mole policing" (Ratcliffe 2016: 5); crime dots appear, and police commanders respond by ensuring activity dots appear on top of them. This pressure to respond to recent crime trends funnels from the top, through district-level commanders, and down to officers in the field. Foot patrol officers knew they had to produce activity to demonstrate that they were doing their jobs and not shirking the department mission. This was obvious during our time walking with officers in Philadelphia. For example, consider the following diary entry:

> They also expressed that they are very bored with their job assignment. "Nothing changes, we see the same people, deal with the same crap. It gets old." They also believe this is why they are unable to get activity, which the Captain has been pushing them to get. "How are we supposed to generate activity when we are confined to the same place, without a car, where everyone knows we are around?" I asked these officers if they were judged by their strong rapport with the community and they explained that there was no way to quantify it, so they are not. They seem to have become increasingly bitter with footbeat work, and looked forward more than ever to being placed in a car. Through my time with them, they did write two parking violations, which they explained is the one way they are able to justify their existence.

Even officers that initially started working beats that were busy had, by the end of the Philadelphia Foot Patrol Experiment, grown bored as criminal activity they could action seemed to disappear. During one observation in West Philadelphia, a field researcher jotted the following:

> "They're (footbeats) boring as hell." I asked what they would rather be doing (already knowing the answer) and they stated that they wanted to be put into regular patrol squads and patrol in cars. They were looking to be involved in action, and believed that, for the most part, foot patrol did not offer the kind of excitement they could experience in a car. They also felt like they weren't helping the neighborhood much anymore, because they're presence was well known, and that people no longer commit crime in their beat. I asked if this was a good thing, and they thought that it was, but staying in the area now offered no benefit.

Later on in this field diary entry, the researcher noted that:

> They told me stories about how exciting it was when they first arrived on the beats, because people did not know they were coming, and didn't expect them to be walking around on foot. They thought that it was no longer as exciting since everyone knew they were there.

Interestingly, these two separate pairs of officers achieved the organizational mission, which was to reduce crime at hot spots via targeted foot patrols. Yet this wasn't enough. Success at a core organizational mission was ironically deemed a personal failure. In other words, officers felt they prevented crime and disorder to the level where they were effective in one respect, but this robbed them of the opportunity to demonstrate productivity and activity, which in turn left them ~~able~~ to the criticism that they were ineffective. Officers felt that they still had ~~~~ to generate activity for their captains to demonstrate that they were doing their jobs. This was true to the extent that some officers were acutely conscious of this inherent conundrum, as evidenced by the following excerpt from field notes:

> One officer seemed to be very insecure. He complained that the other officers think that they aren't doing anything (in terms of making arrests). [The] officer continued that it's difficult to make arrests because there's not a lot of activity on their beat. [The] officer stated that they focus on maintaining a positive relationship with the community. He would find some residents for me to talk to. I mentioned that the purpose of my presence was not to conduct interviews of residents but to observe. [The] officer continued that he wanted me to see how the residents felt about their presence. Therefore, much of the time was spent seeking residents willing to talk to me about the police officers.

In introducing this chapter, we questioned whether foot patrols that emphasized community-oriented policing could properly function within a professional police organization that was more focused on activity that demonstrated traditional crime-fighting outcomes. This quote captures our concerns. Although the officers reportedly engaged in high-quality community work, they lamented their inability to generate activity. In order to prove to us (academics there to simply observe) that they were in fact working, they went out of their way to find community members who could vouch for them. Officers felt pressure to take law enforcement action even when their gut instincts were telling them that exercising discretion would be more appropriate. Consider the following field note:

> They did express a concern with their ability to be community oriented while balancing the enforcement activity numbers that their Captain looks for. They felt bad about writing parking summonses to residents, but stated that if they didn't, it would look like they were doing nothing. I asked if they were gauged at all by their interactions with the community or if the Captain or any supervisor had taken notice of the community relations they had, and they stated that nobody has and probably nobody will ever know. Since their activity sheet doesn't include this, they felt the only way to get recognized was to write tickets, make arrests etc. Despite this, they tried to balance both, and they both thought that the two aspects were equally important.

This is evidence of a common contradiction that many street officers articulate. In a Compstat-type environment, managers and mid-level commanders are able to examine outputs, such as records of arrests, field investigations, and issued tickets. These outputs too frequently become the universal measure of success, rather than community expectations or absence of crime and disorder. Our findings have been noted by others, such as Willis and Mastrofski (in press: 12, emphasis in original) who observed that "officers felt their organisation undervalued the *quality* of their work performance in favour of the *quantity* of their performance. In terms of their career prospects, they believed that their organisation allowed quantity to trump quality, a situation at odds with their personal belief." Officers feel the pressure to provide enforcement metrics as evidence of working, even though they recognize the value of community contacts and how discretion can fuel closer police-community relations. Consider the following interaction from another pair of officers in a different district in Southwest Philadelphia drawn from our field notes:

> They said that since they work the same beat every day they get to know a lot of the residents, which makes it difficult to be very enforcement oriented. They felt bad writing parking violations because they had befriended (at least in a work sense) many of the people. In writing summonses in their own beat, they thought it would detract from their relationship with the residents. With that being said, they wrote a vehicle a parking violation for expired inspection stickers. I asked what kind of pressure they were under to bring in activity, and they said that it was dependent upon the mood of their supervisors that week. They were very candid in explaining that some days they get word that the Captain wants one thing and the next he wants another. I asked if this had anything to do with Compstat, and they weren't sure, but by the way they described it, I surmised it to be in response to Compstat.

Given that we learned that a positive relationship with the community was not only a beneficial outcome of foot patrols on its own but that it also had the ability to generate intelligence, this tension between community policing and a managerial expectation of enforcement is problematic. Clear directives from management and policies that allow for leeway in gauging activity measures for officers performing community work could lessen this pressure to produce for the sake of producing. As Ericson (1982: 28) pointed out nearly 30 years before our first experiment in Philadelphia, "Patrol officers are more likely to concentrate on measurable areas of proactive enforcement ... if they are explicitly rewarded for doing so." The challenge in Philadelphia—as with many places—is the absence of reliable measurement tools around community policing-type interventions. Activity recording systems focus too heavily on enforcement activities and are largely silent on all of the good work officers do in building community relationships and meeting with the community in formal and informal settings. When all that is measured is enforcement, it is not surprising that commanders look to this for their evaluation of street officers. Failing to measure, encourage, and reward positive community interactions is one of the great failings of the modern police management world.

## The Need to Leave: Difficulties Maintaining Beat Integrity

From the perspective of experimentalists, beat integrity, or what we have referred to as "boundary adherence" (Sorg et al. 2014), is critical in order to accurately estimate the crime reduction benefits of place-based policing interventions. Because of the way that crime reduction benefits, crime displacement, and the diffusion of crime control benefits are measured, accurate measurement is enhanced significantly when police stay within the beats to which they are assigned and do not patrol locations outside of their hotspot boundaries. In our studies, it was important that locations that acted as controls should have received little-to-no foot patrol presence. Further, in order to accurately estimate whether crime was displaced to the streets immediately surrounding the intervention sites, officers should not have allowed their presence to spill over into buffer zones that surrounded their beats.

Buffer zones are locations that evaluators use to compare changes in crime from before to after an intervention relative to control locations. They are oftentimes the two blocks adjacent to a targeted location's boundary, adjusted for environmental conditions and the local criminal environment (Ratcliffe and Breen 2011). Using two-block buffer zones, it is possible to document changes in the level of crime at the streets nearby relative to control locations and discern whether there is evidence of crime displacement (crime went up in the streets nearby relative to controls) or a diffusion of crime control benefits (crime went down in the streets nearby relative to controls).

When we asked officers to draw the boundaries of the location that they patrolled during the Philadelphia Foot Patrol Experiment, they drew areas that went well beyond those initially drawn for them. In fact, these "active beats" (Sorg et al. 2014: 379) were on average 0.13 square miles larger than the beats they were assigned to police leadership. All of the locations that were operationalized as buffer zones were patrolled to some extent by the officers. Even some of the control sites (18 of the 60) inadvertently recorded some activity from foot patrol officers.

Given the autonomy afforded foot beat officers, some flexibility in geographic assignment is to be expected. Furthermore, some of the control site activity relates to police work they encountered going between their assigned beat and the police station. We certainly do not suspect any malicious intent because we never publicized the control locations. In an academic evaluation sense, this lack of beat integrity can be a detriment to an evaluation's accuracy, which we have discussed elsewhere (Sorg et al. 2014). What is more of interest here is why did officers leave their beats, and, practically, does it matter that they strayed from their assigned beats now and then?

For many officers, the answer to the first question isn't that deep. They were bored. Officers involved in both of our experiments spent their entire 8-hour shift constrained to only a few street blocks. In addition, many officers reported a noticeable decline in criminal activity within their beats as time progressed. By the tail end of the experiment, a lack of beat integrity was apparent, and a lot of this can be attributed to boredom. The following diary entry from August 2009 was one of many that captured boundary noncompliance as a result of officer boredom toward the end of the experiment:

> As we walked I noticed that these officers were off their beat a lot, and I asked them why this was. They explained that it was small and they were getting bored with it, so after a while they go off to see what's going on in the outskirts. They also felt that people knew they were working it, so there was less and less going on within it. They thought they should be able to move in and out at their discretion because they are there every day and they see what's going on, and what changes are taking place.

The Koper curve seems relevant here. While analyzing data related to observations during the Minneapolis Hot Spot Experiment (Sherman and Weisburd 1995), Koper (1995) explored how long it took for initial deterrence to decay. That is, he sought to understand how long officers were effective at deterring crime before criminals began reoffending. He found that after about 15 minutes, the deterrent effect of police patrols wore off. In Philadelphia, officers were assigned to hot spots for their entire 8-hour shifts. The experiment intended to provide up to 16 hours of police presence each day per beat, well over the amount of time that the Koper curve suggests is optimal. If deterrence is the main objective of a foot patrol program, then it may be that the dosages applied in the Philadelphia Foot Patrol Experiment were unnecessary. The policy implications of Koper's (1995) findings are that police patrols can be effective if short term (about 15 minutes), random, and intermittent, so as to introduce an element of surprise and convey that police are omnipresent and could show up to patrol at any time. That being said, the Philadelphia Policing Tactics Experiment foot patrol component employed fewer officers for less time over larger areas, with no crime reduction effect. So there is definitely a need to expand research in this area to better understand this dosage conundrum.

A number of the officers involved in our experiments reported that offenders had caught on to their patrolling schedules and adapted their offending patterns as a result. Many of these discussions revolved around a perceived temporal crime displacement occurring over time, as noted from the following diary entry from an observer:

> They said that the criminals in the area know their schedules and adapt to them and choose to commit crimes when they are off. They said that in looking at the crime maps, the pattern is apparent, as serious crimes are committed at a heightened rate on their off times.

Another pair of officers was critical of the way in which the foot patrols were being deployed and in fact suggested a deployment scheme that was very similar to what is suggested under the Koper curve:

> These officers were quick to tell me that they believed that they prevent the crime that would occur on their beat were they not there, but felt that criminals have adapted and are aware of their schedules. They were sure that they now come out when they leave and that crime numbers would indicate this phenomenon. It's because of this they felt that the beats should be rotated and others drawn so they could keep criminals 'on their toes' and unsure of where they will be next. They thought the footbeats were a good idea but that they were being implemented improperly.

The Sacramento Hot Spots Experiment has provided some empirical support for Koper's insight (Telep et al. 2014). With this in mind, short, random, and intermittent foot patrols that are rotated across hot spots may be appropriate. However, we ask the reader to recall the benefits of longer-term patrols that we discussed above and further caveat that with the less positive foot patrol findings from the Philadelphia Policing Tactics Experiment. Either way, considering officer boredom and the possible ramifications of this in terms of operational outcomes is useful.

In addition to perceiving that temporal displacement was occurring, many officers believed that their presence caused spatial displacement. There are good theoretical reasons to believe that spatial displacement is not inevitable, theoretical reasons that have been empirically supported through research (Ratcliffe and Makkai 2004; Weisburd et al. 2006; Guerette and Bowers 2009). In the few cases where displacement occurs, the amount of displacement is minimal and less than the crime that was reduced at the target location. In other words, the net effect of the intervention was still positive even after taking into account the amount of crime displaced—as was the case during the Philadelphia Foot Patrol Experiment.

Nevertheless, it is difficult to argue with officers that displacement is not inevitable when they believe that they directly witness it on a recurring basis. Indeed, discussion of spatial crime displacement often arose during our time with officers. They erroneously perceived that it was so problematic that it completely wiped out any benefit that the foot patrols had. One field researcher noted that "They believe that it [foot patrol] prevents crime within the small area their beat is, but not in general. They think that there is a displacement effect, and they don't believe this [foot patrol] has any benefits."

Some of this may be a simple matter of geography. Officers posted to area A may see certain offenders in their area on and off during their shift patrolling just area A. After some time, officers get bored and patrol surrounding areas such as area B, where they see the same offenders. They naturally assume that they displaced the offenders to this location. It is, however, entirely possible that the offenders, throughout the course of the week, occupy both places and have always spent some time at area B. When the officers start patrolling area B, they think the natural occupation of that place by the offenders, who have been going there on and off for years, is the result of being displaced by the officers. Sometimes it is, but this shouldn't be a blanket assumption.

Either way, many officers felt the need to chase down this displaced criminal activity, which inevitably brought them outside of their beats. One officer described to a field researcher the game of "cat and mouse" that he and his partner played with a group of prostitutes:

> [T]he officers said that they were able to chase off a large number of prostitutes that previously frequented the area before they started their patrol. One officer suggested that after they were moved to a new district next week the prostitutes would just come right back. He said that there were a few relentless street walkers in the area, and he was sure that these ladies would call the rest back once they knew the cops were not going to be around to harass them anymore. The other officer compared dealing with prostitution as a "cat and mouse game." He said, "they move around the corner, so we patrol that area …They move a little farther, so we patrol a little farther."

We have previously labeled the spread of a policing treatment outside of the areas intended to be targeted as "dosage diffusion" (Sorg et al. 2016). As we have described above, dosage diffusion can result for a number of reasons. In a practical sense, it seems unlikely that officers occasionally straying from their beat boundaries every now and then would have any meaningful negative consequences; however, findings from our exploration of dosage diffusion using data from the Philadelphia Foot Patrol Experiment suggested that this occurred with greater frequency as the experiment progressed. In other words, as the experiment continued, officers started to stray more often. We also found in a separate analysis that the impacts of the Philadelphia Foot Patrol Experiment declined in places that were staffed for longer periods of time (Sorg et al. 2013). Although we explained these findings through the lens of Sherman's (1990) theory of initial deterrence decay, it may be that dosage diffusion could explain some of these declining effects. If officers were off their beat more often, their deterrent effect is likely to have been diminished as time went on. For commanders wishing to ensure ongoing crime control and disorder prevention in a specified area for the entirety of the operational time period, proper supervision may be essential to avoid dosage diffusion and ensure beat integrity.

## Conclusions

Foot patrol is not as straightforward a practice as it might seem. Officers that were kind enough to allow us to accompany them shed light on the many intricacies of foot patrols and how they might impact program success. These rookie officers struggled to balance enforcement activities with a more community-centered approach to policing. They perceived a pressure to engage in traditional enforcement and policing tactics at times when they would have otherwise used their discretion. As their time on foot beats wore on, they became bored and frustrated with having to remain in boundaries that they perceived as being too small and unable to provide enough activity for them to make their mark. It should be clear after reading this chapter that it is worth explicitly listening to line officers performing the work. Doing so would allow command staff to address some of the numerous concerns that arose during our observations with officers.

Foot patrols are unique in that community members seem perpetually supportive, officers have the potential to generate intelligence as they gain the trust of the community, and as we learned from the Philadelphia Foot Patrol Experiment, they have the potential to prevent crime as well. Their ability to achieve both increased satisfaction among the community and crime reduction benefits will depend upon how foot patrols are utilized, but we believe that they can achieve both outcomes if officers are given the autonomy to address the unique criminogenic and community circumstances that each hot spot presents. Concerns over the need to generate activity can easily be overcome by clear orders and through abandoning the dated practice of gauging officer effectiveness with traditional crime-fighting measures. These, and other policy suggestions, are addressed in the final chapter that follows.

## References

Bittner, E. (1967). The police on skid-row: A study of peace keeping. *American Sociological Review, 32*(5), 699–715.

Ericson, R. V. (1982). *Reproducing order: A study of police patrol work*. Toronto: University of Toronto Press.

Groff, E. R., Johnson, L., Ratcliffe, J. H., & Wood, J. D. (2013). Exploring the relationship between foot and car patrol in violent crime areas. *Policing: An International Journal of Police Strategies and Management, 36*(1), 119–139.

Groff, E. R., Ratcliffe, J. H., Haberman, C. P., Sorg, E. T., Joyce, N., & Taylor, R. B. (2015b). Does what police do at hot spots matter? The Philadelphia policing tactics experiment. *Criminology, 53*(1), 23–53.

Guerette, R. T., & Bowers, K. J. (2009). Assessing the extent of crime displacement and diffusion of benefits: A review of situational crime prevention evaluations. *Criminology, 47*(4), 1331–1368.

Haberman, C. P., Groff, E. R., Ratcliffe, J. H., & Sorg, E. T. (2016). Satisfaction with police in violent crime hot spots using community surveys as a guide for selecting hot spots policing tactics. *Crime & Delinquency, 62*(4), 525–557.

Herbert, S. K. (1997). *Policing space: Territoriality and the Los Angeles police department*. Minneapolis: University of Minnesota Press.

Johnson, L. T. (2016). Drug markets, travel distance, and violence: Testing a typology. *Crime & Delinquency, 62*(11), 1465–1487.

Koper, C. S. (1995). Just enough police presence: Reducing crime and disorderly behavior by optimizing patrol time in crime hot spots. *Justice Quarterly, 12*(4), 649–672.

Lum, C. (2009). Translating police research into practice. *Ideas in American Policing, 11*, 1–15.

Lum, C., & Nagin, D. S. (2017). Reinventing American policing. *Crime and Justice, 46*(1), 339–393.

Mastrofski, S. D., Weisburd, D., & Braga, A. A. (2010). Rethinking policing: The policy implications of hot spots of crime. In N. A. Frost, J. D. Freilich, & T. R. Clear (Eds.), *Contemporary issues in criminal justice policy* (pp. 251–264). Belmont: Wadsworth, Cengage Learning.

Ratcliffe, J. H. (2015). *Harm-focused policing*. Ideas in American Policing. Washington, D.C.: Police Foundation.

Ratcliffe, J. H. (2016). *Intelligence-led policing* (2nd ed.). Abingdon: Routledge.

Ratcliffe, J. H., & Breen, C. (2011). Crime diffusion and displacement: Measuring the side effects of police operations. *The Professional Geographer, 63*(2), 230–243.

Ratcliffe, J. H., & Makkai, T. (2004). Diffusion of benefits: Evaluating a policing operation. *Trends and Issues in Crime and Criminal Justice, 278*, 1–6.

Ratcliffe, J. H., Taniguchi, T., Groff, E. R., & Wood, J. D. (2011). The Philadelphia Foot Patrol Experiment: A randomized controlled trial of police patrol effectiveness in violent crime hotspots. *Criminology, 49*(3), 795–831.

Ratcliffe, J. H., Groff, E. R., Sorg, E. T., & Haberman, C. P. (2015). Citizens' reactions to hot spots policing: Impacts on perceptions of crime, disorder, safety and police. *Journal of Experimental Criminology, 11*(3), 393–417.

Sherman, L. W. (1990). Police crackdowns: Initial and residual deterrence. In M. Tonry & N. Morris (Eds.), *Crime and justice: An annual review of research* (Vol. 12, pp. 1–48). Chicago: University of Chicago Press.

Sherman, L. J. (1998). *Evidence-based policing*. Washington, D.C.: Police Foundation.

Sherman, L., & Strang, H. (2004). Experimental ethnography: The marriage of qualitative and quantitative research. *The Annals of the American Academy of Political and Social Science, 595*(1), 204–222.

Sherman, L., & Weisburd, D. (1995). General deterrent effects of police patrol in crime "hot spots": A randomized, controlled trial. *Justice Quarterly, 12*(4), 625–648.

Sorg, E. T., Haberman, C. P., Ratcliffe, J. H., & Groff, E. R. (2013). Foot patrol in violent crime hot spots: Longitudinal impacts of deterrence and post-treatment effects of displacement. *Criminology, 51*(1), 65–101.

Sorg, E. T., Wood, J. D., Groff, E. R., & Ratcliffe, J. H. (2014). Boundary adherence during place-based policing evaluations: A research note. *Journal of Research in Crime and Delinquency, 51*(3), 377–393.

Sorg, E. T., Wood, J. D., Groff, E. R., & Ratcliffe, J. H. (2016). Explaining dosage diffusion during hot spot patrols: An application of optimal foraging theory to police officer behavior. *Justice Quarterly*, 1–25.

Telep, C. W., Mitchell, R. J., & Weisburd, D. (2014). How much time should the police spend at crime hot spots? Answers from a police agency directed randomized field trial in Sacramento, California. *Justice Quarterly, 31*(5), 905–933.

Thacher, D. (2001). Policing is not a treatment: Alternatives to the medical model of police research. *Journal of Research in Crime and Delinquency, 38*(4), 387–415.

Weisburd, D., Wyckoff, L. A., Ready, J., Eck, J., Hinkle, J. C., & Gajewski, F. (2006). Does crime just move around the corner? A controlled study of spatial diffusion and diffusion of crime control benefits. *Criminology, 44*(3), 549–591.

Willis, J. J., & Mastrofski, S. D. (in press). Improving policing by integrating craft and science: What can patrol officers teach us about good police work? *Policing and Society*.

Wood, J. D., Sorg, E. T., Groff, E. R., Ratcliffe, J. H., & Taylor, C. J. (2014). Cops as treatment providers: Realities and ironies of police work in a foot patrol experiment. *Policing and Society, 24*(3), 362–379.

Wood, J. D., Taylor, C. J., Groff, E. R., & Ratcliffe, J. H. (2015). Aligning policing and public health promotion: Insights from the world of foot patrol. *Police Practice and Research, 16*(3), 211–223.

# Foot Patrol Policies

## Introduction

The most pertinent question any police commander contemplating deploying foot patrol should ask themselves is "What do I want to achieve?" This seems like a trite comment, but foot beat officers are frequently deployed without real clarity on what it is hoped they will accomplish. Clear and specific goals for a foot patrol operation are therefore essential. Even though the research evidence described earlier in this book is somewhat mixed, it is clear that foot patrols have the potential to achieve a myriad of policing goals. When Moskos wrote about New York City's Operation Impact—a massive foot patrol program started in 2003 and involving up to 1800 rookie officers—he concluded "If the goal of police is to prevent crime, and it should be, foot patrol is the answer. Impact works" (Moskos 2008: 202). The Philadelphia Foot Patrol Experiment also found that, with sufficiently enthusiastic officers in small, high-crime areas, violence could be reduced (Ratcliffe et al. 2011). Furthermore, the officers developed a considerable understanding of the local criminal environment and of local people on the margins of society (Wood et al. 2014). That being said, the Philadelphia Policing Tactics Experiment a year later discovered that reducing the dosage and making the foot beat areas larger negated any impact (Groff et al. 2015). These variable findings seem to mimic the limited research evidence from the preceding decades. Crime reduction is possible but not guaranteed. Foot patrols are not a silver bullet that can be applied in any random fashion. They should be a tailored and targeted strategy, suitably resourced, and with coherent and reasonable goals. Simply copying a deployment strategy from another police department carries little risk for a police chief and is easily justifiable if the original department claims success, but it will often fail because the two departments police areas with different problems, politics, officers, and communities.

It's also clear that—whether effective at crime reduction or not—the public seem to adore foot patrols. When, during the Newark Foot Patrol Experiment, foot beats were added to neighborhoods that had not had foot patrol in the preceding 5 years,

© The Author(s) 2017
J.H. Ratcliffe, E.T. Sorg, *Foot Patrol*, SpringerBriefs in Criminology,
DOI 10.1007/978-3-319-65247-4_5

the communities perceived their areas to be the safest with the lowest likelihood of victimization, and they were not only aware of the foot patrols but also improved their evaluations of the job done by the police department (Pate 1986). Even in cities like Baltimore, where the police department and community have had a somewhat strained relationship in recent years, communities still request foot patrol to help deal with drug trafficking issues[1] (U.S. Department of Justice 2016) and have successfully lobbied for foot patrols in troubled areas of the city (West Baltimore Commission on Police Misconduct and the No Boundaries Coalition 2016: 5).

If used judiciously and in the right locations, foot patrol, therefore, appears to have the potential to reduce crime, reassure the community, improve perceptions of the police department, and gather criminal intelligence. These are, however, very different tasks that will most likely require consideration of the geographic area, selecting the right type of officer, a different type of briefing and instructions to the officers (how officers are tasked), and a different type of reward system. This chapter discusses each of these considerations.


## Selecting the Right Officers

In December 2004, then Secretary of Defense Donald Rumsfeld told CNN that you go to war with the army you have, not the army you might want or wish to have at a later time. The same could be true of policing given that few police leaders in the field are also responsible for recruitment and training. In some circumstances and departments, operational commanders will be assigned officers for foot patrol without any choice in the matter. For example in Philadelphia, new officers—rookies—spend their first few months on foot patrol, and in New Haven, Connecticut, new officers out of the academy spend a year on foot patrol (Cowell and Kringen 2016). However, outside of these types of mandatory programs, a local area commander may have at least some discretion in selecting officers within his or her command for specific duties. If so, what are the characteristics of a good foot patrol officer?

Again it is worth reiterating that most pertinent question for a local commander has to be "what do you want to achieve?" The types of police officer drawn to community policing, helping the homeless, or working in gang interdiction or street crimes units are all probably different in significant ways, with personalities that reflect these different interests. As Moskos noted, "In high-crime neighborhoods everywhere, most police don't give a damn about community relations. Officers tend to scoff at community relations in part because the 'community' police deal with are mostly criminals" (Moskos 2008: 203). Selecting officers with the wrong mix of skills may be disastrous for the outcome of a project. If the objective is to use foot patrol to improve community perception of police legitimacy, no amount of

[1] A request that was not granted unfortunately and a source of complaint by the community. See page 156 of U.S. Department of Justice (2016) *Investigation of the Baltimore City Police Department*. Civil Rights Division. 10th August, 2016

patrol will make any difference if the officer's attitude toward community interaction is hostile. For example, consider the views of the Department of Justice officials after their interviews with officers in the Baltimore (MD) Police Department:

> We found a prevalent "us-versus-them" mentality that is incompatible with community policing principles. When asked about community-oriented problem solving, for example, one supervisor responded, "I don't pander to the public." Another supervisor conveyed to us that he approaches policing in Baltimore like it is a war zone. A patrol officer, when describing his approach to policing, voiced similar views, commenting, "You've got to be the baddest motherfucker out there," which often requires that one "own the block." (U.S. Department of Justice 2016: 157)

The fundamental mind-set of the officers is likely to be the most important factor; however, it is also worth considering the career stage of potential foot patrol officers. After nearly 20 years' ethnographic work with the Los Angeles Police Department, Barker (1999) contextualized police careers in 5-year blocks, with each stage representing an evolution of experiences, attitudes, and behaviors. It is likely that officers in their first few years are likely to approach foot patrol very differently than veterans not far from their pensions.

A survey of 400 officers from a variety of US police departments examined the productivity of police officers in these different career stages across a range of proactive measures; the number of traffic citations issued, DUI arrests made, and the number of drug arrests effected. The research confirmed what many in policing intuitively suspected. Officers in their first 5 years were highly motivated and productive, and by the time they were in their second career increment (5–10 years), they hit their stride and productivity was maximized (Johnson and LaFrance 2016). This is most likely due to a combination of having "learned the ropes" and how to orient themselves around operational systems, developing the confidence to conduct proactive police work, and having gained the experience necessary to be effective and efficient. After 10 years, productivity declined in the surveyed officers, possibly due to burnout, disgruntlement, or disengagement to focus on interests external to policing (Barker 1999).

If commanders seek to use foot patrol to reduce a substantial crime problem and feel that enforcement and proactive activity is a route to that goal, then assigning officers who are younger in service would appear prudent. They are likely to be more motivated to engage in proactive police work. As many of the rookie foot beat officers in Philadelphia told us, they wanted to work hard, try different styles of policing, and try to come to the notice of their superiors in a positive way. If the desired outcome is enhanced community relations, then selecting older officers with more service and a desire to be more community service oriented might be a more appropriate strategy. While they may be a little more cynical of the police organization and more averse to engaging in proactive work, they might welcome the opportunity to work with the community and develop contacts with people that are not grounded in conflict. The identification of late-career opportunities for officers may be a useful way to keep them engaged and to retain their experience and professional knowledge. As Dempsey argues, more seasoned officers may be able to exercise better judgment and discretion when dealing with incidents and radio calls.

And while good judgment is important for all patrol officers, foot beat officers are particularly visible to the community (Dempsey 1992).

Whomever commanders select, the officers will be more enthusiastic if there is clear and explicit evidence from the precinct/district leadership that foot patrol is valued as distinct from other operational roles. This requires that commanders set realistic goals and targets for the foot patrol officers and objectives that are more in line with the reality of a foot post. Assessing the merit of foot patrol officers against the outputs of vehicle-bound officers (such as number of calls attended or arrests made) would appear to be counterproductive and misses the value that foot patrol can bring to a community and crime reduction strategy.

Officers who "get" the change of pace and focus of foot patrol and are willing to keep working actively even if they are no longer in a rapid response role and mind-set should be encouraged to volunteer for foot patrol. Moskos (2008: 203), while on foot patrol with the NYPD during Operation Impact, recognized that "Foot patrol is tedious and tiring. And as if to confirm foot patrol's low organizational status, only rookies are assigned to Impact. While the theory behind Operation Impact itself has been described as 'Compstat on steroids,' actually doing it can be as boring as listening to a statistician on Quaaludes." It therefore requires officers with the right mind-set, officers who are at least willing to engage in public interaction. When out walking with two Philadelphia foot patrol officers in the 22nd district, author Dan Rubenstein (2015: 77–8) noted this interaction between "cops and robbers" thus:

"What happened?" a fleshy young man said to [police officer Brian] Nolan and his partner, Mike Farrell, as they walked past. "Somebody steal your car?"

"Just getting some exercise," Nolan shot back. "You might want to try it sometime."

The above is hardly the epitome of a civil exchange but potentially important in terms of starting an interaction that could be of benefit to crime prevention. The officer has made eye contact and will no doubt remember the same young man next time he comes around the block. With the injection of a little humor, an olive branch of connection might be possible. At the very least, the young man is probably more aware that the officer can recognize him in the future and can find out who he is. Something this simple can help the crime reduction effort. After all, crime loves anonymity.

Rocco Urella, who was serving in 1971 as the Pennsylvania state police commissioner, noted that "with a policeman with the *basic right attitude* on the beat you are going to get public support. Public support is the necessary element in effective police enforcement" (Grimes 1971: 3, emphasis added). The challenge is identifying and rewarding the basic right attitude. One of the simplest ways to get on the right track of the basic right attitude is to request volunteers. If a project and its goals are outlined, requesting volunteers can attract officers with the right attitude and mind-set because they know what the project entails before they volunteer. Of course, this may initially be a challenge. Across the five departments studied by Cowell and Kringen (2016), they noted how many of the foot beat officers did not initially want to be on foot patrol. Only after experiencing the work directly did the officers see the benefits to the community and to themselves.

When we interviewed officers during the Philadelphia Policing Tactics Experiment, there was quite a gulf in attitude and enthusiasm between foot patrol officers who volunteered and those who didn't. At times, we heard from officers who had been either ordered to the foot beat or "voluntold" (told they were volunteering or ordered to volunteer). They often reported being bored by the work and thought the project a waste of time. Volunteers appear much more willing to go beyond doing the minimum and were keen to learn more about the particular crime problems in the beat from crime analysts and the community. They would come into the university and speak enthusiastically about what they did and what they hoped to achieve. The difference in attitude and perception of the job was jarring.

## Training Foot Patrol Officers

In the wake of the successful Philadelphia Foot Patrol Experiment, the Philadelphia Police Department instigated a policy that placed every new officer from the academy on a foot beat for the first few months of their service. In the wake of that policy, a training document noted that "This document was prepared with the realization that most of us received little training on how we should walk a foot beat, or what tactics we should employ while assigned to one" (Philadelphia Police Department 2010: 1).

If a commander seeks to address a significant crime problem and thinks that officers on foot can better target serious repeat offenders, then training in the latest rules and requirements regarding pedestrian stops and field investigations is vital. Officers on foot probably have a better capacity to argue for a totality of circumstances regarding why they stopped and frisked an individual than officers in cars because they are more in tune with the neighborhood, its problems, and the crime issues in the area. Furthermore, they are often more likely to have observed the specific behaviors of a suspect for a longer period of time than officers who pull up in a car. While the pace of foot patrol is slower, it allows more time to observe suspicious behavior, appreciate situations and contexts, and gather reasonable justification for actions. The rules regarding the Fourth Amendment to the Constitution of the United States appear to be frequently misunderstood by officers, so a legal update and instruction on how to clearly articulate the circumstances of every stop are important.

If officers are to be more than walking enforcement machines and engage with a community problem-solving role, then it has been noted that:

> Officers assigned to foot patrols must have the training, resources, and support to develop and implement programs that address the specific needs of the beat area. Initiatives could include school presentations designed to curb underage drinking, physical security assessments to decrease the likelihood of crime, coordination of other departmental resources such as traffic or narcotics to address an identified problem, or supporting crime watch groups. (Craven 2009: 1)

One officer in Philadelphia used these skills to request the posting of "no loitering" signs, and when posted "this gave him probable cause to stop those who were causing problems or hanging out on the sidewalks. After some time, the problem disappeared" (Philadelphia Police Department 2010: 2).

A third area where training can be helpful is in the area of social assistance and public health. Rather than see a snapshot view of a situation, officers on a permanent beat assignment can develop a longitudinal view of the problems affecting people and places that have been referred to as "microplaces of harm" (Wood et al. 2015: 218). In urban environments, this often brings officers into contact with people struggling with drug addiction and mental health issues. The reality is that even if officers do not embrace the role:

> Law enforcement officers, and especially foot patrol police, serve as public health interventionists, despite the fact that this role is incidental both to the imagination of officers and the general public. In the course of their daily routines, foot patrol police encounter health risk behaviors and environments, yet there are improvements to be made both at the level of police knowledge and attitudes, and more broadly at the city level where coordinated efforts to bridge security and health are critically needed. (Wood et al. 2015: 220)

Awareness of addiction and treatment options, as well as training in dealing with people struggling with mental health issues and cooccurring issues, will be valuable to officers if these are significant issues in the proposed foot patrol environment.

## The Geographic Area for Foot Patrol

If the aim of foot patrol is to reduce crime, then the geographic area should have a significant concentration of crime. Foot patrol is just one technique of many that falls under the rubric of hot spots policing. It has long been known that crime is more concentrated in some places than others (Guerry 1833; Quetelet 1842; Mayhew 1862), and in the urban milieu crime focuses in small places known as "hot spots" (Spring and Block 1988). These hot spots are places that are a geographic area of higher than average crime relative to nearby locations (Chainey and Ratcliffe 2005; Eck et al. 2005). Crime hot spots can vary from street to street (Weisburd et al. 2004), and even within high-crime neighborhoods, crime can cluster at specific locations, yet the contiguous areas remain relatively crime-free (Sherman et al. 1989). Hot spots policing is the focusing of police resources and crime prevention activities to these higher-crime places. If police are to have a deterrent effect on crime, then it has been argued by numerous researchers that the best return on the investment in policing should be found in the places where crime is most concentrated (Braga 2005; Weisburd and Braga 2006; Braga et al. 2012).

It does, however, also depend on the type of crime. Shoplifting, by its very nature, is an indoor activity usually conducted away from the surveillance of officers patrolling the public street. The same can be said for other crimes that are usually conducted indoors or in other nonpublic places, such as non-stranger rape, credit card fraud, and assaults in schools. Foot beat officers are more likely to be effective against street crimes such as vehicle theft or theft from vehicles, residential and nonresidential burglary, robberies, assaults, and public disorder events. Some research has identified a threshold level of crime below which it may be difficult to demonstrate any statistically significant impact of hot spots policing. For example, the Philadelphia Foot Patrol Experiment identified a minimum threshold of around six incidents in the preceding 3 months (i.e., in the top 40% of beats) as a baseline violent crime indicator that the hot spots were active enough to benefit from an intervention (Ratcliffe et al. 2011). In a hot spots policing experiment in Sacramento (California), a minimum threshold of 30 calls for service in the preceding 90 days was identified as a significant indicator of likely hot spots policing success (Mitchell 2016; Telep et al. 2014).

If the operational commander's desire is to improve community relations, then it may be possible to select a larger beat that contains a number of places where people gather for work or social events. The Newark Foot Patrol Experiment areas had about 150 to 200 households and on average between 35 and 50 nonresidential places like churches, schools, and businesses (Pate 1986). A better return on the investment of foot patrol in terms of improving public perception of the police may be possible if the officers focus on areas where the public congregate and more citizens can see their officers. Possible examples include outside of schools at school opening or closing time, in or near public transit intersections (especially during rush hours), and near places of worship. These are all good places for officers to "circulate and mingle." Places with higher concentrations of residents are particularly helpful, such as walking through public housing schemes and projects and attending community meetings and events. If businesses are being targeted for crime or for general reassurance purposes, then foot patrols that concentrate on the business corridor in question are also appropriate.

## Hot Spots Within Hot Spots: The Hotspot Matrix

Business districts can become a sort of "hot spot within a hot spot," a characteristic of some crime areas previously recognized over a decade ago and articulated through the Hotspot Matrix. The Hotspot Matrix is a typology of spatiotemporal characteristics of hot spots that categorizes the potentially infinite array of spatiotemporal arrangements into three broad categories of within-hotspots spatial patterns and three broad categories of temporal pattern (Ratcliffe 2004). It becomes operationalized when an analysis identifies the type of crime distribution that is occurring within a crime hot spot. So even though the general area is known to be a high-crime one, are the individual crime events scattered throughout the crime hot spot (a *dispersed* spatial pattern), do they demonstrate some spatial clustering (a *clustered* pattern), or is there a particular place (such as a bar or school) that is responsible for the vast majority of the crime within the hot spot (a *hotpoint*)?

The Hotspot Matrix also has broad categories for temporal patterns. As stated earlier, both authors bring personal experience of police foot patrol to this book. For example, one of us (Ratcliffe) can still remember being posted to the Roman Road Market in Bow, East London back when it was in the old H district of the Metropolitan Police. A foot patrol in the vicinity of a busy street market that had suffered numerous vehicle thefts and thefts of items from cars probably seemed a good idea. After all, offenders were taking advantage of busy market times and the influx of vehicles that were left unsupervised while market stall owners worked the market and customers visited the area. But given that the market was only open a couple of days a week and always deserted by 5 pm, a weeklong night shift walking patrol in the market area from 10 pm to 6 am seemed particularly ill-conceived and pointless. Awareness of time is therefore important in any deployment.

Analysts and command staff should therefore ask "what is the temporal signature of the crime events within the hot spot?" The Hotspot Matrix suggests three main temporal patterns. If "the crime events could happen at any time over the 24-hour period of a day, or because the time span of events is so large that it is not possible to determine any significant peaks of activity" (Ratcliffe 2004: 11), then the temporal pattern is described as *diffused*. Note that the time span refers to the possible range of times in which a crime could have occurred. Assaults are usually easy to identify, having a short time span based on the victim knowing when he or she was assaulted; however, burglary and vehicle theft can have long time spans, comprised of the time between when the victim last saw the property unmolested and the time when the crime was discovered.

There may be a temporal signature when crime is *focused*. This means that crime could occur at any time of the day but tends to have a shorter period of a few hours when there is significantly more crime activity. After school hours or business districts vulnerable to overnight burglary are good examples of *focused* temporal patterns.

Finally, the last category is "a rare group of hotspots where the temporal activity is confined to a small period of time, or where the [temporal] signature almost negates the possibility of criminal activity at some time periods. This does not mean that some events cannot occur in other periods, except that unlike the focused hotspot, there are few events happening outside the acute time" (Ratcliffe 2004: 12). These acute temporal patterns can occur at troublesome bars around closing time or outside sports stadiums after a game.

As an example, consider Table 1 which shows an example Hotspot Matrix for a commander considering the use of foot patrol to deal with a street crime problem in an urban community. Within the crime hot spot itself, the temporal pattern could be *diffused* (crime could occur any time of the day or night) and the spatial pattern *dispersed* (anywhere within the hot spot). With such a *diffused*, *dispersed* hot spot, foot patrol would have to tour the entire crime hot spot at all hours of the day and night. This would require teams of foot patrols, increasing cost and reducing likely effectiveness. Compare the operational possibilities to a crime hot spot that had a robbery problem that was temporally *focused* and spatially *clustered*, such as in the area immediately around a small commercial strip in the hours after schools let out.

**Table 1** An example Hotspot Matrix for using foot patrol in an urban community

| Hotspot Matrix for foot patrol tackling an urban community street crime problem | | Spatial patterns | | |
|---|---|---|---|---|
| | | Dispersed | Clustered | Hotpoint |
| Temporal patterns | Diffused | Probably unfeasible or ineffective | Potentially effective but expensive | Likely highly effective |
| | Focused | Potentially effective but expensive | Potentially effective | Likely highly effective and cost-efficient |
| | Acute | Potentially effective | Likely effective and cost-efficient | Likely highly effective and cost-efficient |

With such a *focused, clustered* hot spot, officers would know where to concentrate their activities, and the commander would not have to make the foot patrol a 24-hour a day assignment. This increases likely effectiveness and efficiency of cost— increasing the likelihood that the foot beat officers can make inroads into the crime problem.

## Other Foot Beat Area Considerations

What about more suburban or rural areas? As Moskos (2008) suggests, a good rule of thumb could be that if the mail carrier is delivering the mail on foot (therefore mainly urban and suburban locations), then it should be possible to patrol on foot. Many dormitory suburbs in America are spatially dispersed, and they frequently lack footpaths. These would be difficult and probably less effective places in which to conduct foot patrol. So while an initial scan of a jurisdiction might identify a hot spot in rural and suburban areas with lower population densities, these hot spots can be awfully large areas for foot patrol to cover. With a lower density of crime often the result, the benefits are likely to be minimal in terms of crime reduction and potentially below a threshold of any value at all (Mitchell 2016). The crime patterns should be closely monitored for some form of spatial and temporal pattern before committing resources in suburban or rural areas. Bicycle patrols may be an alternative to consider in areas that are deemed too large for traditional foot beats.

It has been our experience that a police commander's initial instinct is frequently to make a foot beat area as large as possible, in the hope of maximizing the crime or reassurance rewards of the commitment of resources. This is usually a mistake. Larger areas increase the diversity of the foot beat and increase the ratio of places within the patrol grid that have little crime. It also reduces the impact of any community reassurance. If people see officers walk down their street every 15 minutes, then they know they are in a foot patrol area. If they see officers walk down their street only once, they probably suspect it is a peculiarity. Any offenders in the area are unlikely to adjust their perception of risk that the police will interdict if they commit an offense. Again, if an area is deemed too large, bicycle patrols may be a viable alternative.

It should be borne in mind that officers have demonstrated a tendency to stray from their assigned locations. To minimize this, great care should be taken to include sufficient areas in the beat to make it interesting, while keeping it as small as possible. This point is also dependent on the crime problem. For example, if a nuisance bar is central to the crime problem, then the bar should, of course, be included in the beat. But consideration should be given to including nearby parking lots if bar patrons park there or to local transit stops. Incorporating a local drug market or commercial strip will provide additional ways for officers to stay constructively busy.

One possibility is to design pilot foot beats and then revise them a couple of weeks after they have been implemented. If the commanders include the operational officers who are actually working the street in any redeployment discussion, then the experiences of the officers can be incorporated into an improved design that will more closely mirror the underlying pattern of human behavior and physical environment. It will also improve the commitment of the officers to the target area.

## Tasking Foot Patrol Officers

There is some evidence suggesting that selecting officers for foot beats who are starting out and new to the job results in more use of enforcement sanctions. As one sergeant who worked in New York's Operation Impact said "A lot of rookie cops go to the worst areas and just attack: write summonses, write everything, arrest everybody" (quoted in Henderson 2015). In Philadelphia, we discovered this during the Philadelphia Foot Patrol Experiment when pedestrian stops, arrests, and other types of enforcement increased significantly in the intervention areas (Ratcliffe et al. 2011). One Philadelphia police captain described a recent success in a violent crime gang hot spot by stressing the value of foot patrols: "Deployment wise, we increased our deployment, we increased our visibility in that area, we got some feet on the ground. .. We got foot beats down there and constantly hit that area" (Haberman 2016). While on the surface, this can sound proactive, in our experience, officers are often dispatched to a crime hot spot with insufficient information to enable them to perform optimally. How are officers supposed to achieve the goals of their commanders if those same leaders do not pass on sufficient instructions? It sounds trite, but both of the authors of this book have seen it happen time and time again. Commanders want to address a particular issue and build community support but don't convey those key details to the foot patrol officers. The foot beats do the best they can but sometimes engage their role in a way that is counterproductive to the commander's intent.

At the very least, officers (in any capacity—not just foot patrol) should be made aware of the reason for their assignment and how they are supposed to best support the organization and their commander's mission. They might receive a few pointers from the sergeant on roll call, but too often the sergeant is equally unaware of the dynamics of the crime problem and leadership's intent. Information that was discussed in a management meeting (such as crime briefings or Compstat meetings) is rarely conveyed effectively downward through the ranks. As a result, foot patrol officers receive a geographic assignment with little additional information beyond that there has been a spike in robberies, for example, in the general area. Does the commander want the officers to engage with the community, or conduct surveillance on known offenders, or provide reassurance patrols in busy areas? Commanders rarely articulate their goals or the measures by which success will be assessed. This presents a wasted opportunity to maximize the use of an expensive resource, often leaves inexperienced officers to determine tactics, and can result in officers feeling disillusioned when they do not see any amelioration of the problem they are trying to address. The foot patrol officers can feel like they have been "dumped" in an area, divorced from the organization, and undervalued.

Good goals for foot patrol should be SMART goals: specific, measurable, achievable, realistic, and time-bound. By setting these types of objectives, the application of foot patrols to address a policing problem becomes more accountable. In other words, by having specific and measurable goals that have an identified time frame (when will the goals be achieved?), it is possible to evaluate the outcome. Although evaluations may expose failed policies, the identification of when something is not working is usually the necessary catalyst to improvement (Syed 2015).

Foot patrol need not only be about enforcement for short-term crime reduction gains (where they can be achieved). After all, "foot patrol is a protean concept that serves many masters while achieving many goals" (Giannetti 2007: 22). Some innovative commanders have used foot patrol as a mechanism to gain useful information and intelligence on community problems. In Philadelphia, one entrepreneurial police officer assigned to a crime analysis role gave surveys to the foot patrol officers assigned to her district. The survey responses identified key features of the community's residential design that were enabling a burglary problem to continue and thrive. This officer (since promoted) saw an opportunity to gain more community intelligence by using foot patrols as more than just tools of community engagement or enforcement.

In a 2010 survey of over 100 officers in Philadelphia, nearly two-thirds thought that patrol officers (in general, not just foot patrol) effectively use their knowledge of activities going on in their beat to reduce crime, and more than three-quarters felt that patrol officers have the skills and ability to collect information on their beats (Ratcliffe et al. 2012). During Philadelphia's Operation Safe Streets, foot patrols provided sufficient criminal intelligence such that, once the foot beats reverted back to vehicle patrols, one commander lamented "the intelligence that was supposed to be recorded on the officers' supplemental logs –intelligence vital to the redirection of patrol efforts—had dried up" (Giannetti 2007: 26). Yet when given the option of expanded patrols in high-crime areas, the officers in the 2010 Philadelphia survey

**Table 2** VOLTAGE analytical framework

| VOLTAGE | Example questions |
| --- | --- |
| Victims | Does crime concentrate among a certain type of victim or target? Are there multiple victims or is a particular target the subject of frequent victimization? Does the type of target generate particular public concern (such as children)? |
| Offenders | Is the crime spike created by numerous offenders who are not known to each other? Is it caused by a few repeat offenders? Are there new offenders in the area (such as prison releases)? |
| Locations | Are specific places targeted, or is crime distributed more widely? Is a crime hot spot caused by a hot point, or is crime dispersed within a crime hot spot? |
| Time | Is the crime spike within normal variation or explainable by annual seasonal patterns? If not, are there specific times when crime is concentrated? Are new patterns evident? |
| Attractors | Are particular locations or places attracting offenders because of the easy criminal opportunities (attractors), or are places inadvertently creating crime opportunities (generators)? Where are the top worst places? |
| Groups | Are gangs or intergang conflicts a factor in the crime spike? Is there involvement of organized crime? Are school children involved either as offenders or victims? Are there disputes between criminal families and fans of particular sports teams? |
| Enhancers | Are factors such as drug or alcohol use a factor to consider? Are behavioral (mental) health issues part of the problem? |

Source: Adapted from Ratcliffe (2016: 123–4)

preferred other patrol types. While 55% thought foot patrol would be effective or very effective at combating violent, more supported bicycle patrol (73% effective or very effective) and vehicle patrol (79% effective or very effective). The effectiveness of bicycle patrols is largely unknown, but it is increasingly clear that motorized patrols do not gather much information useful to crime analysis or criminal intelligence.

If information collection is one goal of foot patrol, or even a part of a larger strategy, then one potential framework for tasking officers is VOLTAGE. VOLTAGE is a structured analytical framework designed to provide a configuration to analytical questions within policing (Ratcliffe 2016). VOLTAGE is shown in Table 2 and has its origins in an intelligence-led policing framework for understanding crime problems. Crime analysts may be able to help address some of the components of the VOLTAGE framework; however, foot patrol officers are uniquely placed to build local relationships and interact with people on the street in a way that can facilitate a deeper and more insightful understanding of the area's crime problems. Regretfully, in too few instances do we find that foot patrol officers are used to gather information that can inform a comprehensive crime reduction response.

We have witnessed foot beat officers (at the behest of crime analysts) go business-to-business speaking to store owners and assessing their willingness to help with a crime reduction initiative, survey burglary victims and gather more information about local crime, and work closely with transit officials to learn more about the link between crime in a train station and the surrounding areas. In Philadelphia, two foot patrol officers "created a book in which they have information on all those who have active warrants, past criminal histories, and those who they ped stop in their beat. They collect and update this information on a regular basis. They explained that being well informed and studying this information is necessary because criminals are constantly studying them. Their tactics have 'leveled the playing field.'" (Philadelphia Police Department 2010: 3). While these initiatives appear to be rare examples, they demonstrate potential. And importantly from the first example, there is no point gathering information "just in case it's needed." It must be delivered to someone who can use it to improve decision-making (like a commander or crime analyst).

If foot patrol officers are assigned goals that are specific to the problem they are being tasked to address, they can then be held accountable to those goals. This then opens up the possibility of assessing the value of foot patrol on a more expansive range of criteria relevant to public safety and security.

## *Permanent or Park-and-Walk Patrols?*

Rather than initiate permanent foot beats, some police departments have started to mandate that officers get out of their patrol car on a regular basis and walk in the community. These programs can be traced back to the *stop, walk, and talk* initiatives in places like Baltimore County (Maryland) in the early 1980s (Hayeslip and Cordner 1987). In St. Petersburg, Florida, the program is called *Park, Walk, and Talk*, and it requires all officers in the St. Petersburg Department to park in a neighborhood and chat to local people there for one hour a week (Bekiempis 2015). To ensure compliance, officers must log this activity so that participation can be confirmed by supervising officers. In early 2015, the Baltimore Police Department mandated that every officer gets out of their car at least once during a 10-hour shift, for a period of at least 30 minutes—a program that even had the support of the police union (Bekiempis 2015). However command staff do not enforce the mandate or provide sufficient supervision, so in reality, few officers actually comply. An official review concluded "It is, therefore, unsurprising that some officers fail to integrate community policing efforts into their time on patrol. There are few incentives and little encouragement to do so" (U.S. Department of Justice 2016: 161).

Sometimes these issues with maintaining foot patrol are due to a lack of organizational and cultural commitment with the department. At other times, they are related to realistic resource constraints. As one foot patrol officer interviewed in the study by Cowell and Kringen (2016: 28) lamented, "Staffing ruins everything—if you don't have enough bodies, the walking beats are the first to go—they'll pull you out of the walking beats and put you somewhere else." Walk-and-talk programs may therefore be a genuine attempt to introduce foot beats while also a response to limited resources.

These different types of program have not been tested experimentally, so we cannot say for sure whether they are effective. As social scientists, we are reluctant to draw any conclusions from inconclusive (or nonexistent) data, but we also know this is the kind of vacillation that annoys practitioners seeking some indication of best practice. We will therefore offer an opinion based on our extrapolation from the limited existing knowledge.

The problems with limited and temporary programs where officers are encouraged or mandated to talk to the community for an hour a week or an hour a day are numerous. First, we are concerned that the amount of dosage is so small as to have no noticeable impact on either crime or community sentiment. One hour a week, here and there, is probably unlikely to change the perception of risk in the minds of would-be offenders nor will it improve the crime risk perception of potential victims. Second, there is probably insufficient dosage to convince a community that the police department is really investing in community policing in their area. Third, one hour per week (or similar) is probably insufficient time for officers to get into the appropriate mind-set for the change in pace and policing style. If they are spending the other 39 hours of their workweek in a traditional vehicle-based response role, one hour per week of park and walk is probably just viewed by most officers as a necessary evil designed to provide nothing more than merely a gesture to the community. And the community may see it the same way, perceiving a lack of true commitment by the police department.

Of course, it may be that a department is willing but strapped for officers and resources and unable to instigate a permanent patrol in a high-crime area. So is a temporary patrol strategy better than nothing? Perhaps, but this would need to be confirmed with a suitable experimental study. And considerable work may need to be made to convince the officers and the community that the effort is more than a "crowd-pleaser." Split shifts (four hours in a car, four hours on foot) might be way to test the effectiveness of a higher dosage without committing resources to foot beats permanently and might be an ideal strategy for a department with vehicle shortages.

## Incorporating Foot Beats into an Area's Overall Crime Control Strategy

One frequent finding in the research literature is the relative isolation of foot patrols from their colleagues organizationally. Consider the following from Skogan and colleagues discussing the Chicago Alternative Policing Strategy in the 1990s:

> As we observed in many areas, important contributions were made by the district's foot patrol officers. In Fiesta they were particularly enthusiastic about problem solving, and they were repeatedly singled out for praise by community activists. Foot patrol officers were also in close contact with the area's thriving business community and available by pager. However, as we also frequently observed, they were not considered part of the beat team, did not attend team meetings, had no role in the beat's implementation plan and were not asked to attend beat community meetings that occurred off their shift (Skogan et al. 1999: 205)

Similarly in the (unnamed) southeastern city of the United States that introduced foot beats to a business area, subsequently studied by Esbensen, the foot patrol officers met with the local area commander, meeting separately from their patrol comrades (Esbensen 1987). There can surely only be benefits if patrol officers in a response capacity are aware of the goals of the foot patrols and can provide appropriate support where necessary, and in return, foot beats can pass on information which may have an intelligence value to their colleagues in motorized patrol. Separate briefings seem to set up an unnecessary divide, and we feel is indicative of a lack of strategy integration at the local level.

A second consideration is the length of time for a foot patrol deployment. More than one study has found a decay in foot patrol effectiveness over time. In Philadelphia, our research into the foot patrol experiment found a decay in effectiveness started during the deployment and progressively got worse during the course of the program. Foot patrol became less effective over time (Sorg et al. 2013). A similar decay was found in the Kansas City Foot Patrol Project (Novak et al. 2016). After 90 days, regression models showed that the foot patrol implementation did not have a statistically significant impact on the number of aggravated assaults and robberies in each area over the entire period of the project. However as noted earlier, the coefficients were in the right direction, and there was no evidence of displacement or a backfire effect (things did not get worse). The researchers did identify an initial impact in the early phase of the foot beat implementation that was statistically significant. This might suggest the sort of treatment decay that was observed in Philadelphia. As the researchers concluded, "an examination of violent crime revealed statistically significant reductions in crime in the micro-places receiving foot patrol treatment, although the deterrent effect quickly decayed," going on to write "foot patrol need not (and should not) be implemented for the long term, but, rather, may be usefully implemented for relatively short periods." They estimate 6 weeks as a potential deployment length. It may be that nonpermanent patrols that last a number of weeks are more effective if moved around on an unpredictable basis than having permanent deployments that drag on for months and months with little sign of effectiveness.

## The Community Component

While arguing for the use of crime mapping to aid deployment, Craven (2009) adds that foot patrols will be successful with a full involvement of the community in the patrol priorities. She goes on to suggest that departments "recruit a range of individuals (both officers and civilians) to use various models of patrol, demonstrating that both police and civilians can address public expectations through a variety of approaches such as volunteer efforts with neighborhood watch programs and crime-prevention programming." That might be a bridge too far for some police services; however, her point that foot patrol officers are serving a community support role appears clear. As we pointed out in the introduction to this book, a key component—perhaps the core value of foot beat officers over vehicle patrols—is the ability for officers to be more approachable. Mackenzie and Whitehouse (1995) note that police officers on foot were viewed as approachable by the public, and they found that officers who patrolled on foot alone were deemed as more approachable than officers who patrolled in pairs. The belief that foot beat officers are more approachable has been confirmed by focus groups of the community and foot patrol officers (Cowell and Kringen 2016).

In our 2010 survey of over 100 officers in Philadelphia, many of the survey results were encouraging for the development of community policing. For example, only 7% of officers disagreed (or strongly disagreed) with the statement "police officers should work with the citizens to try and solve problems in their beat," just 10% disagreed—strongly or otherwise—with the statement "improving the relationship between the PPD and the community is a priority of mine," and only one person disagreed that "police officers should make frequent informal contacts with the people in their beat" (Ratcliffe et al. 2012). Yet in the same survey, more officers disagreed than agreed with the statement "The [police department] should spend more time getting to know minority communities" and the modal groups were neutral with regard to "The community in my patrol area is appreciative of my presence."

The challenge with incorporating a community policing element into foot patrol policing is knowing the activities on which to focus. Community policing has been variously described as "a collaboration between the police and the community that identifies and solves community problems" (CPC 1994), as "a philosophy that promotes organizational strategies, which support the systematic use of partnerships and problem-solving techniques, to proactively address the immediate conditions that give rise to public safety issues such as crime, social disorder, and fear of crime" (U.S. Department of Justice n.d.: 3), or as "an organisational strategy that leaves setting priorities and the means of achieving them largely to residents and the police who serve in their neighbourhoods" (Skogan 2006: 27–28). With such vague definitions, it is clear that community policing can incorporate a myriad of activities including school visits, neighborhood watch, D.A.R.E. training, newsletters, coffee-with-a-cop-type meetings, community meetings, and participating in neighborhood events. Foot patrol officers in Cambridge, Massachusetts, hand out slushy tickets to kids, and in New Haven, Connecticut, they hand out their cell phone numbers to people to improve community contact (Cowell and Kringen 2016). In many regards, the fluidity in the elements that people conceive as community policing has led to "fruitless debates" over what constitutes community policing (Mastrofski 2006: 44).

The challenge in an evidence-based policing framework is how to assign meaningful community activities to foot patrol officers, given there is little evidence to support the efficacy (either way) of any specific individual activities at improving crime prevention, public perception of crime risk, or perceptions of police legitimacy. Most police departments engage with all of these activities, mainly through dedicated community liaison officers rather than foot patrol officers. They are probably undertaken with a tacit acknowledgment that all of these tasks may have some undefined value, and therefore they had better do them all, just in case. But if we are to improve the rationale for policing and become more effective and efficient through evidence-based policing, at some point each action and role should individually come under the microscope if we are to disentangle the values of each and ultimately justify the ongoing use of taxpayer funds. And if foot patrol officers are tasked with community support activities, then the mechanisms for reward and accountability should reflect these roles. This challenge is discussed in the next section.


## Assessing and Rewarding Foot Patrol


As part of his Ph.D. dissertation, Cory Haberman interviewed Philadelphia police district command staff. He wanted to know how they addressed crime in their districts and conceptualized solutions to crime problems. One Philadelphia police captain noted, "When they [potential offenders] see the cops all around here, cops on a bicycle, cops on foot, they may go elsewhere." Another told Haberman, "My foot beats were off yesterday, I drove by [intersection], all the junkies were on the corner, all the drunks were on the corner. You know, you go by when the foot beats are in there, they're gone" (Haberman 2016). Clearing corners may be an important activity in terms of public safety, but—as described above—does not necessarily generate arrest statistics or even field interview reports. In Cambridge, Massachusetts, foot patrol officers resolved a public nuisance issue in a manner that didn't involve an arrest or law enforcement:

> The department was receiving numerous complaints about homeless individuals sitting on milk cartons and loitering in front of businesses. One of the foot patrol officers figured out that these individuals were taking the milk cartons from the very businesses that were making the complaints because those businesses were not locking up their storage rooms. That officer went around to all of the businesses and arranged for the businesses to lock up their storage rooms, and the problem subsequently ceased. (Cowell and Kringen 2016: 11)

How then should the value of these actions be assessed, and if it does help to reduce disorder and violence, how do we reward officers for making the additional effort? The generating of statistics has been hugely important in the Compstat environment of New York City (Eterno and Silverman 2006; McDonald 2002), but the nuances of minor community contacts and the role they play in the potential to reduce crime have yet to be explored by criminologists. And approaches like Compstat can drive short-term thinking (Ratcliffe 2016), especially in police departments that have a quota expectation, whether it is formal or informal. Quotas "insult police professionalism and contribute to community hatred of the police. In a quota-driven system, police tend to see all citizens, even the good ones, as potential stats" (Moskos 2008: 206). Increasingly, both patrol officers and command staff recognize that these traditional measures of productivity are irrelevant to the myriad goals of foot patrol assignments (Cowell and Kringen 2016).

At a macro level, if cities are well resourced and have the incentive to do so, regular community surveys can help gauge community sentiment. Craven suggests departments "Complement statistical analysis with a community survey to obtain the opinions of residents and business owners regarding priority issues [and] invite the community to participate in planning sessions" (Craven 2009: 1). Community surveys cannot be one-off events. Individual surveys represent a mere snapshot of community sentiment; however, when multiple surveys are completed, it is possible to determine how community perception of crime and the police is changing over time. This ability to determine a trajectory of community satisfaction is more valuable than a single survey point. This requires cities and police departments to commit to multiple years of surveys and to retain the same questions across those years so that a true comparison can be made.

A possible future alternative to community surveys is the measurement of community sentiment via social media such as Twitter. There is evidence that Twitter data is correlated with reported crime counts, though there are still multiple sources of bias and error in these data (Williams et al. 2017). This is a relatively new area, and at the time of writing, there is little solid and reliable information on how to robustly measure community sentiment using social media. However, it does represent an emerging area that might in the future be able to reduce the costs of gathering public perception without the expense of community surveys. With geolocated tweet activity, it may be possible, in the future, to measure changes in public perception of crime risk or at the microlevel of geography at which foot patrol functions.

## Conclusion

In this chapter, we have endeavored to coalesce the available evidence and opinions available on best practice for the reader. We have tried to stay within the bounds of the available knowledge, but unfortunately, in many cases, there is simply an absence of robust research to support a policy one way or the other. In other words, we simply do not know what does and does not work in terms of best practice because too few departments have set up foot beats in a way that makes them amenable to study or opened their departments to the possibilities of research. Our conclusions, therefore, come with an important caveat that some of the views are based on our opinion, well known to be the lowest form of viable evidence (Farrington 2003). Many of our recommendations cannot be implemented individually. For example, an assurance from the top has to be met with enthusiasm from rank-and-file officers. As Moskos (2008: 207) notes:

> A long-term commitment is needed for foot patrol to reclaim its place as the dominant form of patrol. At the top, the pressure to produce stats needs to let up. The only stats that matter— and they should be related— are crime, fear, and satisfaction. For police officers, foot patrol must be seen as real police work. That change needs to start at the bottom. If the transition to foot or bike isn't voluntary, the anti–foot patrol mentality will never change.

With these important caveats in place, our policy recommendations from this chapter can be summarized as follows:

## Objectives

- Commanders should establish clear goals for the foot patrol operation.
- Officers should be briefed on their specific goals and objectives.
- Briefing of foot patrol should take place alongside other (non-foot) patrols.
- Occasional foot patrol (for a brief period during a shift) has not yet been demonstrated to be effective.

## Recruitment

- Officers should be selected based on their personality for the intended role.
- Volunteers should be sought whenever possible.
- Younger officers may be appropriate when enforcement activities are desired.
- Late-career officers may be more suited to community engagement.

## Area Selection

- If the local mail carrier does not walk, then the area may not be suitable for foot patrol.
- Smaller beats encompassing only a few streets appear to be more effective than larger areas that dilute any positive effects.
- Adjusting beats after they have been operational for a time to avoid deterrence decay seems prudent.
- Deploying via the spatiotemporal signature of the problem (via the Hotspot Matrix) may increase efficiency.

## Demonstrating a Return on the Investment

- Specific training for the desired role is important, especially with regard to legislation around pedestrian investigations, dealing with people with drug or behavioral problems, and accessing other city support services.
- Information gathering should be emphasized, and that information should be collated by someone.
- Measuring community sentiment before and after foot beat deployment may be as helpful in demonstrating the value of the officers' deployment as crime statistics.
- Where possible, foot beats should be operationalized so their effectiveness can be tested.

This last point is important for policing. The constraint running through this entire book is the lamentable absence of robust evaluation regarding foot patrol, an absence that hampers the identification of appropriate best practice. Until more police departments are prepared to try different approaches, test them, be prepared for them to not work, and then adapt to better strategies, we will never truly learn how to best deploy foot patrol—or any other tactic. Policing will remain mired in the limited value of experience, opinion, and guesswork.

# References

Barker, J. C. (1999). *Danger, duty, and disillusion: The worldview of Los Angeles police officers.* Prospect Heights, IL: Waveland Press.

Bekiempis, V. (2015, May 17). Foot patrol: A catch-22 of community policing. *Newsweek.*

Braga, A. A. (2005). Hot spots policing and crime prevention: A systematic review of randomized controlled trials. *Journal of Experimental Criminology, 1*(3), 317–342.

Braga, A. A., Papachristos, A., & Hureau, D. (2012). *Hot spots policing effects on crime. (Campbell systematic reviews no. 8).* Oslo: Campbell Collaboration.

Chainey, S., & Ratcliffe, J. H. (2005). *GIS and crime mapping.* London: Wiley.

Cowell, B. M., & Kringen, A. L. (2016). *Engaging communities one step at a time: Policing's tradition of foot patrol as an innovative community engagement strategy.* Washington, D.C.: Police Foundation.

CPC. (1994). *Understanding community policing: A framework for action.* Washington, D.C.: Community Policing Consortium.

Craven, K. (2009). Foot patrols: Crime analysis and community engagement to further the commitment to community policing. *Community Policing Dispatch (The e-newsletter of the COPS Office), 2*(2), e-newsletter.

Dempsey, T. (1992). *Contemporary patrol tactics.* Englewood Cliffs: Prentice Hall.

U.S. Department of Justice. (n.d.). *Community policing defined.* Washington, D.C.: Office of Community Oriented Policing Services.

Eck, J. E., Chainey, S., Cameron, J. G., Leitner, M., & Wilson, R. E. (2005). *Mapping crime: Understanding hot spots* (p. 79). Washington, D.C.: National Institute of Justice.

Esbensen, F.-A. (1987). Foot patrols: Of what value? *American Journal of Police, 6*(1), 45–65.

Eterno, J. A., & Silverman, E. B. (2006). The New York city police department's compstat: Dream or nightmare? *International Journal of Police Science and Management, 8*(3), 218–231.

Farrington, D. P. (2003). Methodological quality standards for evaluation research. *Annals of the American Academy of Political and Social Science, 587*(1), 49–68.

Giannetti, W. J. (2007). What is operation safe streets? *IALEIA Journal, 17*(1), 22–32.

Grimes, S. (1971). *Foot patrolmen losing out to red cars.* Philadelphia Bulletin. Feb 4th.

Groff, E. R., Ratcliffe, J. H., Haberman, C., Sorg, E., Joyce, N., & Taylor, R. B. (2015). Does what police do at hot spots matter? The Philadelphia policing tactics experiment. *Criminology, 51*(1), 23–53.

Guerry, A.-M. (1833). *Essai sur la statistique morale de la France: Precede d'un rapport a l'Academie de sciences.* Paris: Chez Crochard.

Haberman, C. P. (2016). A view inside the "Black Box" of hot spots policing from a sample of police commanders. *Police Quarterly, 19*(4), 488–517.

Hayeslip, D. W., Jr., & Cordner, G. W. (1987). Effects of community-oriented patrol on police officer attitudes. *The American Journal of Police, 6*(1), 95–119.

Henderson, B. (2015). A night on patrol with the NYPD. Newsweek. 6th June 2015.

Johnson, R. R., & LaFrance, C. (2016). The influence of career stage on police officer work behavior. *Criminal Justice and Behavior, 43*(11), 1580–1599.

Mackenzie, I. K., & Whitehouse, R. (1995). The approachability of police officers patrolling on foot: A pilot study. *Policing and Society, 5*(4), 339–347.

Mastrofski, S. D. (2006). Community policing: A skeptical view. In D. Weisburd & A. A. Braga (Eds.), *Police innovation: Contrasting perspectives* (pp. 44–73). Chicago: Cambridge University Press.

Mayhew, H. (1862). *London labour and the London poor.* London: Griffin Bohn.

McDonald, P. P. (2002). *Managing police operations: Implementing the New York crime control model – CompStat.* Belmont: Wadsworth.

Mitchell, R. J. (2016). *The Sacramento hot spots policing experiment: An extension and sensitivity analysis.* Unpublished dissertation, University of Cambridge, Cambridge.

Moskos, P. (2008). *Cop in the hood: My year policing Baltimore's Eastern District.* Princeton: Princeton University Press.

Novak, K. J., Fox, A. M., Carr, C. M., & Spade, D. A. (2016). The efficacy of foot patrol in violent places. *Journal of Experimental Criminology, 12*(3), 465–475.

Pate, A. M. (1986). Experimenting with foot patrol: The Newark experience. In D. P. Rosenbaum (Ed.), *Community crime prevention: Does it work?* (pp. 137–156). Newbury Park: Sage.

Philadelphia Police Department. (2010*). Foot patrol: Our veterans' perspectives.* http://www.smartpolicinginitiative.com/sites/all/files/Foot%20patrol%20training%20document.pdf. Accessed 8/3/2016.

Quetelet, A. (1842). *A treatise in man.* Edinburgh: Chambers.

Ratcliffe, J. H. (2004). The hotspot matrix: A framework for the spatio-temporal targeting of crime reduction. *Police Practice and Research, 5*(1), 5–23.

Ratcliffe, J. H. (2016). *Intelligence-led policing* (2nd ed.). Abingdon: Routledge.

Ratcliffe, J. H., Taniguchi, T., Groff, E. R., & Wood, J. D. (2011). The Philadelphia Foot Patrol Experiment: A randomized controlled trial of police patrol effectiveness in violent crime hotspots. *Criminology, 49*(3), 795–831.

Ratcliffe, J. H., Groff, E. R., Haberman, C. P., & Sorg, E. T. (2012). *Smart policing initiative final report (Unpublished)* (p. 92). Washington DC: Bureau of Justice Assistance.

Rubenstein, D. (2015). *Born to walk.* Toronto: ECW Press.

Sherman, L. W., Gartin, P., & Buerger, M. E. (1989). Hot spots of predatory crime: Routine activities and the criminology of place. *Criminology, 27*(1), 27–55.

Skogan, W. G. (2006). The promise of community policing. In D. Weisburd & A. A. Braga (Eds.), *Police innovation: Contrasting perspectives* (pp. 27–43). Chicago: Cambridge University Press.

Skogan, W. G., Hartnett, S. M., DuBois, J., Comey, J. T., Kaiser, M., & Lovig, J. H. (1999). *On the beat: Police and community problem solving.* Boulder: Westview Press.

Sorg, E. T., Haberman, C. P., Ratcliffe, J. H., & Groff, E. R. (2013). Foot patrol in violent crime hot spots: Longitudinal impacts of deterrence and post-treatment effects of displacement. *Criminology, 51*(1), 65–101.

Spring, J. W., & Block, C. R. (1988). *Finding crime hot spots: Experiments in the identification of high crime areas.* 1988 Annual meeting of the Midwest Sociological Society, Minneapolis, 1988.

Syed, M. (2015). *Black box thinking: Why most people never learn from their mistakes - but some do.* New York: Portfolio/Penguin.

Telep, C. W., Mitchell, R. J., & Weisburd, D. (2014). How much time should the police spend at crime hot spots? Answers from a police agency directed randomized field trial in Sacramento, California. *Justice Quarterly, 31*(5), 905–933.

U.S. Department of Justice (2016). *Investigation of the Baltimore City Police Department* (trans: Division, C.R.). (pp. 163). Washington, D.C.: Civil Rights Division.

Weisburd, D., & Braga, A. A. (2006). Hot spots policing as a model for police innovation. In D. Weisburd & A. A. Braga (Eds.), *Police innovation: Contrasting perspectives* (pp. 225–244). New York: Cambridge University Press.

Weisburd, D., Bushway, S., Lum, C., & Yang, S.-M. (2004). Trajectories of crime at places: A longitudinal study of street segments in the City of Seattle. *Criminology, 42*(2), 283–321.

West Baltimore Commission on Police Misconduct, & The No Boundaries Coalition. (2016). *Over-policed, yet underserved: The People's findings regarding police misconduct in West Baltimore* (p. 31). No Boundaries Coalition for Central West Baltimore; Baltimore MD. http://www.noboundariescoalition.com/commissionreport/

Williams, M. L., Burnap, P., & Sloan, L. (2017). Crime sensing with big data: The affordances and limitations of using open source communications to estimate crime patterns. *British Journal of Criminology, 57*(2), 320–340.

Wood, J. D., Sorg, E. T., Groff, E. R., Ratcliffe, J. H., & Taylor, C. J. (2014). Cops as treatment providers: Realities and ironies of police work in a foot patrol experiment. *Policing and Society, 24*(3), 362–379.

Wood, J. D., Taylor, C. J., Groff, E. R., & Ratcliffe, J. H. (2015). Aligning policing and public health promotion: Insights from the world of foot patrol. *Police Practice and Research, 16*(3), 211–223.

# Index

© The Author(s) 2017
J.H. Ratcliffe, E.T. Sorg, *Foot Patrol*, SpringerBriefs in Criminology,
DOI 10.1007/978-3-319-65247-4

CPSIA information can be obtained
at www.ICGtesting.com
Printed in the USA
BVOW07s0822171017
497882BV00003B/7/P